The ABC's of Picture-taking Ease

with the Canon AE-1, AE-1 PROGRAM and AV-1 cameras

Part 1
Part 2
Part 3
Part 4

Production Staff

Author	D.O.D. Inc., as prepared by Dale R. Wright
Publisher	Canon Inc.
Project Manager	Yoji Miyazaki
Coordinator	Masamichi Kakunodate
Art Director	Akira Yonishi
Editorial Design	Yoshinobu Oguchi
Cover Design	Yutaka Harada
Staff Photographer	Hirofumi Gotoh
Illustration	Kazuhiro Yato
Production Supervision	Canon Inc. Canon U.S.A., Inc.
Printer	Nakamura Seiko Printing Co., Ltd.

About the Author

A writer and photographer, Dale Wright received his training at Wittenberg University in the United States and as a foreign student and professional writer in Japan. In his capacity as the chief copywriter for D.O.D. Inc., a Tokyo public relations firm, he has spent the past four years handling and writing about Canon photo equipment. He and Canon have seen each other through introduction of the AE-1, AT-1, A-1, AV-1 and countless accessories.

Printed in Japan

Preface

Although this book was written mainly by one author, the original concept was wholly a Canon Inc. idea. They realized the existence of a demand for such a book from the many present and future Canon camera owners in America. Only a few of the people who participate in the making of a book can ever be mentioned in its pages. We would therefore like to take this opportunity to give special thanks to Jody Wright, wife of the author and a former Canon employee, who acted as unofficial editor and contributed the section "Treating Your Camera Well". We would also like to thank all of the many photographers for allowing us to use their work and various organizations both in Japan and the U.S. who lent us their support. We hope you have as much fun reading this book as we had making it.

With the introduction of the Canon AE-1 PROGRAM, a section is provided herein on the correct handling of this new camera.

Table of Contents

Part 1

Part 2

Part 3

Part 4

Have you purchased a Canon "A" series camera, or are about to? If so, this is the book for you. Perhaps you have noticed Canon TV commercials or magazine ads that tell you how easy it is to get great pictures with your A-1, AE-1, AE-1 PROGRAM, AV-1 or AT-1. Chances are, if you are new to the 35mm camera picture-taking game, your first results were not very encouraging. Maybe you hadn't read your instruction booklet and make a mistake. Maybe you used the wrong film for the shooting conditions. Maybe your lens just wasn't suitable for the kind of picture you desired. Or, maybe manipulation of a camera part would have given a better effect.

This book was written to try and give you basic knowledge about photography and tips on how to handle different situations—technique and equipment-wise. Since the AE-1, AE-1 PROGRAM and AV-1 cameras cater to a broad market, we assume that you are, or are planning to be, an owner of one of them. Thus, all explanations are centered around them. This does not mean, however, that if you have another A series camera, or even one of a different make, you cannot use this book. A good deal of the information actually pertains to general photography; it can be used by the owner of any 35mm SLR camera to improve his photography.

Said simply, the ultimate aim of this book is to erase any frustration you may have encountered in using your expensive, high-technology 35mm SLR camera. Used properly, there isn't any reason why it shouldn't give you the beautiful, awe-inspiring photographs of the professional. Toward that end, the book is divided into four parts. The first one is basically an

introduction just to give you an idea of how influential photography is on our daily lives and how the concept of photography got around to becoming a reality.

Then, the second part delves into the hard part of photography—the principles behind its working. You will learn about such difficult-sounding terms as "film sensitivity", "exposure", "shutter", "aperture", and so on. This section should be read carefully as the knowledge contained therein will form the basis for utilization of the techniques explained later. This section also introduces the Canon photographic system to you and describes the A series of cameras in some detail.

Part Three proceeds to give basic instructions on how to operate the AE-1, AE-1 PROGRAM and AV-1 and two of their dedicated flashes, the Speedlites 188A/177A. And since the FD interchangeable lenses are central to Canon's photographic system, considerable space has been devoted to explaining them group by group. Your selection of them for your own system will make a lot of difference in the kind of pictures you take. Use of the new Power Winder A2 and A are also explained in this part.

Having come this far, you are now ready to apply your knowledge and equipment. But various photographic situations require special techniques. To start off, Part Four describes basic lighting methods and

filters, which are all-important devices used by professionals. Sixteen separate photographic themes are then presented with hints on techniques and equipment given. Most of the major areas and problems that you will encounter have been touched upon. Following these sections are comments on how to display and use your pictures for both commercial and non-commercial purposes, how to take care of your camera and a short history of camera and film development. The

specifications of each A series camera and accessory have also been provided so that you can see the capabilities of these products, with a question-and-answer section at the end of the book.

The sample pictures are all ones that you yourself can do. In the first part of the book they are representative of the most popular types. Towards the end, they get more and more sophisticated, as does your knowledge and experience. But of course, reading the text and looking at the pictures is just one phase of your photographic training. To become really skilled, don't forget the old adage "practice makes perfect."

The field of photography is a broad one. To cover everything it encompasses would necessitate a much bigger book than this. For that reason, things not so popular with amateurs such as black-and-white photography and self-development/printing of film have not been included. If you wish to study about these aspects, or about subjects covered in this book but in more detail, there are many books on the market devoted to various branches and techniques of photography. We only hope that what you glean from this one will give your photography some direction, and make your hobby more interesting and personally fulfilling. That, after all, is what it's all about.

Although you may think the camera is merely a convenient instrument for taking snapshots, its uses are as varied as the colors of a peacock. Newspapers would be far less attractive without the pictures that cover almost every page. And magazines are literally plastered with them. Some, like National Geographic, have enjoyed a high reputation thanks to the excellence of their photography. In fact, general photography has become so widespread that even a lot of high school newspapers use pictures taken (and in some cases developed) by students.

In a different realm, cameras have been sent up to space abroad Apollo, Voyager and other spacecraft to photograph the heavens. And they've gone to the depths of the ocean to take astounding pictures of marine life. Miniature cameras even enter people's bodies, giving doctors a clearer picture of what's going on.

You, too, can be part of this exciting world by experimenting with and perfecting the techniques presented in this book. It may take a little effort and some time, but you'll find it's not as hard as you think.

Part 1

The first man-recorded images and how they sowed the seeds of photography; Background of the modern-day camera; How an image is formed and the function of a lens therein; Description of the modern SLR; A few examples of different kinds of photography.

For eons, indeed ever since the dawn of the human race, mankind has been concerned with images. At first they took crude forms—paintings on walls, inscriptions on animal bones called oracle bones and the like. The former evolved into what we now know as art; the latter formed the basis for a written language now used by almost 1 billion people: Chinese. Both cases were depictions of the way man sees his environment, ways to record what's going on around him.

But writing on walls, engraving characters into bone, or even painting on an easel can be fairly complicated. It took a stroke of pure luck, though, for the principle of an easier method to be found.

It happened ages ago, when an Arab wise man was sitting in the middle of the desert in his tent. He suddenly noticed a spot of light on the wall he was facing, inside of which was something moving. It was his camel that was tied up outside; the sun's rays striking the animal had gone through a hole in the tent just behind the wise man, forming an image on the wall. He didn't really see the significance of it, and it wasn't until centuries later that an Italian picked up the idea and put a lens into the hole to sharpen the image. After that, improvements came fast and furious. Till where the principle has been refined into a precision instrument that modern-day human beings have fallen in love with —THE CAMERA.

There were many important breakthroughs and inventions that led to the modern-day camera. When thinking about how easy it is to take a picture today, some are quite laughable. Like the 1,400 pound behemoth dubbed the Mammoth camera that was built in 1900.

Long before this, however, the principle discovered by our Arab friend had been introduced into Italy by none other than Leonardo da Vinci. The first practical application probably occurred when an Italian scientist, using his house as a so-called camera obscura and improving the image with a lens, invited some friends to have a look. After that, movable chambers were built so that this camera obscura could be taken along to a particular place, the scene of which had to be traced onto translucent paper.

By the way, the Italian scientist's guests, rather than being amazed by the demonstration, actually fled in terror. That's because the image of the hired actors performing outside his house was upside-down; they thought a sorcerer was at work!

The explanation of this phenomenon can be found by turning the page. And if you care to know in more detail the history of photography's development, refer to the back of this book.

In 1839, Louis Jacques Mandé Daguerre completed the first type of photograph, the Daguerrotype. The kind of camera used and sold at that time was one made by Alphonse Giroux called the Daguerrotype Camera.

As you can see from the illustration, light rays coming from two points on the subject fly off in all directions. These two points are of course only for the sake of discussion. Actually, an infinite number of rays bounce off all points on the subject, to say nothing of its surroundings. Without anything to concentrate these rays, no image can be formed because the light rays are all over the place. Here's where the hole in the tent comes into play!

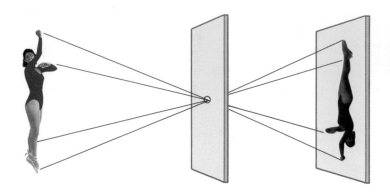

It is so small that only a few rays from each point can enter. The places where they fall are so close together that an image is formed. This hole must be quite small, however, for the bigger it is, the fuzzier the image becomes.

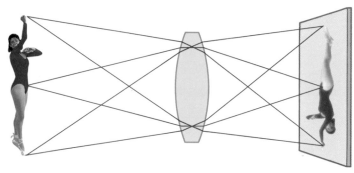

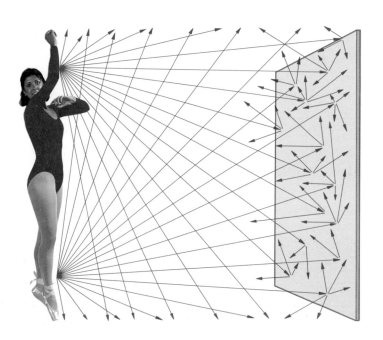

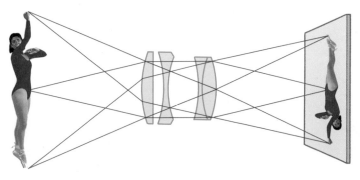

Which is all fine and dandy. But exactly why does the image appear upside-down? The reason lies in the nature of the light rays themselves. Light travels in a straight line, therefore when it is reflected by an object and goes throught the hole, right becomes left, top becomes bottom and vice versa, as shown in the illustration.

Besides the above problem, the camera obscura had definite disadvantages in another respect, too. Since the hole had to be so small, not too much light could enter. At the time photosensitive materials were discovered, one exposure could take a whole working day —eight hours to be exact! Obviously, something was needed that could concentrate great amounts of light, but yet keep the hole small. That certain thing is called a lens.

Clarity with a Convex/Concave Combination

Basically, there are two types of lenses used in modern-day cameras. One is a convex, also called a positive lens, and the other is concave or negative. Use of the former four centuries ago by a Venetian nobleman

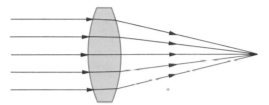

The concentration of light by a convex lens.

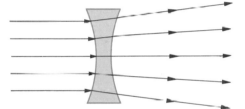

The diffusion of light by a concave lens.

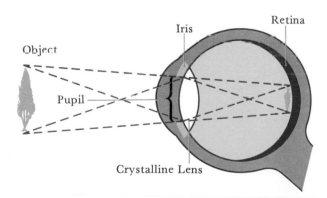

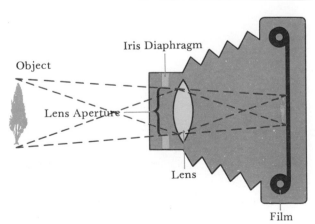

on his camera obscura was a momentous event for photography. The unique characteristic of this lens, which is fatter in the middle than at the edges, is that it collects many rays of light and bends them till they all criss-cross at the same point. This point is known as the focal point and the vertical surface where all these points fall to make an image is the focal plane.

Terminology aside, you have probably discovered by now the advantage of a convex lens. By concentrating many rays of light, rather than only a few as with a mere pinhole, illumination is vastly increased enabling exposure times of fractions of a second. And, of course, the subject becomes comparatively sharp.

But it's still not sharp enough due to the fact that not all colors of a light ray bend at the same angle. Enter the concave lens. Since it has opposite effects (being negative and a diffuser of light), it helps compensate for the fuzziness or chromatic aberration present if only one convex lens is used. To ensure sharp pictures, present-day camera lenses contain a combination of from 4 to 15 concave and convex lens elements. The optical characteristics of each lens determine what combination is used.

Nature's Eye vs. the Camera's

Actually, the lens of a camera "sees" just like a human eye. Its pinhole, or diaphragm (refer to page 46) by which the amount of light entering is controlled finds its twin in the eye's iris. The image that the eye's lens helps form is brought into focus by muscles which thicken or thin the lens. In the camera, the same effect is accomplished by moving the lens back and forth. And the image is fixed by the retina in the human eye, by the film in the camera.

But there's one function neither the eye nor the camera lens can do: make the image rightside-up. The image that the eye picks up is righted by the brain. But the brain cannot compensate for the image that is inverted by the camera's lens. It needs help. That came with the modern-day SLR camera.

You as a photographer have quite a variety of picture-taking instruments to choose from, all with different film formats and camera structures and suited for different purposes. There is the small, fixed-focus type camera which, because of the comparatively poor image it gives, will not even enter into our discussion. The view camera, quite like the old camera obscura but with a compound lens, is used by many professionals. It, however, must be used on a tripod and since the image is viewed directly through its lens, the subject appears upside-down. Or, you can choose a rangefinder camera. It has different optical systems for viewing the scene and taking the picture. So the image won't look like an inverted reflection in the water. The only trouble is, the difference in position of the viewfinder and lens leads to a phenomenon known as parallax error. Result: when you get close to the subject, what you see in the viewfinder will not necessarily be captured on film. In fact, the top of whatever you are shooting will be chopped off. Also, even when you can change lenses (expensive models only, which also have built-in parallax error correction), the scene you see will not change to suit the new lens.

Which brings us to the hero of our story and the subject of this book—the Single Lens Reflex camera, or SLR.

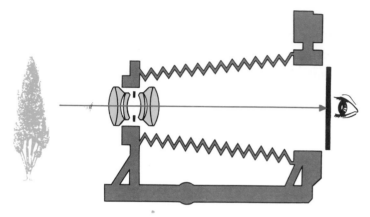

The View Camera

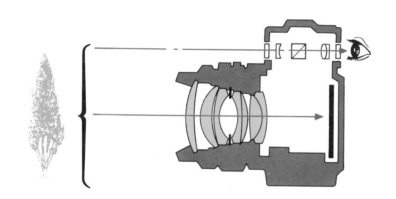

The Rangefinder Camera

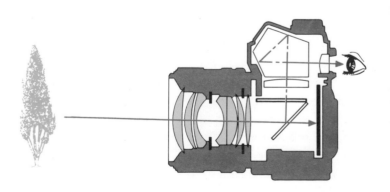

The Single-lens Reflex Camera

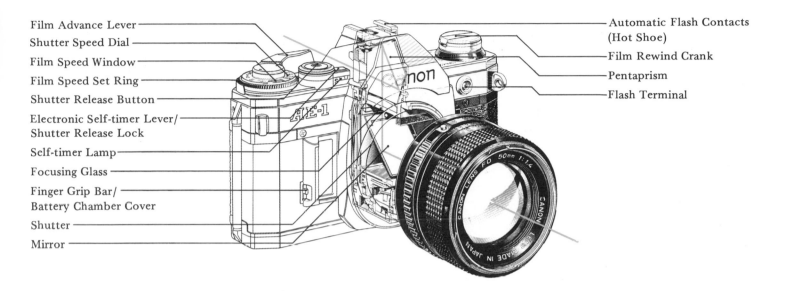

Film Advance Lever
Shutter Speed Dial
Film Speed Window
Film Speed Set Ring
Shutter Release Button
Electronic Self-timer Lever/
Shutter Release Lock
Self-timer Lamp
Focusing Glass
Finger Grip Bar/
Battery Chamber Cover
Shutter
Mirror

Automatic Flash Contacts
(Hot Shoe)
Film Rewind Crank
Pentaprism
Flash Terminal

The SLR is a 35mm camera. What this means is that it uses 35mm cartridge film having a width of 35mm and a picture frame of 24 x 36mm. But more important, this camera is really a miracle of modern technology. First, it has taken care of the inverted image problem by employing a mirror and a device called a pentaprism. This arrangement enables the image that the lens picks up to be seen as is by the photographer and at eye-level. The mirror reflects the image (which is upside-down, remember) up to the pentaprism. There, the image bounces around inside this 5-sided prism and emerges with everything in its right place (top at the top, bottom at the bottom, right side on the right, left side on the left.) But that's not all of the advantages.

Any recent SLR will have a built-in light meter. It used to be that you had to measure the amount of light coming from the subject by a separate, hand-held meter. This was necessary so that not too much or too little light would strike the film and ruin the picture. (Light is allowed to strike the film when the mirror swings up and the shutter opens.) Now, with a built-in meter, you can tell immediately as you manipulate the aperture and shutter speed when the proper exposure is obtained. This somewhat confusing lingo, by the way, is explained further on pages 38—47.
Suffice it to say that this innovation has made photo-

graphy indescribably simpler and more exact. It is especially simple in the AE-1, due to the use of advanced electronics, which we will also get into later.

There's something else about an SLR camera, too, that could make you spend lots of money and think every cent is worth it. They're called interchangeable lenses and they enable you to see exactly what the film records, even when you change lenses. Being able to change them at will is also an important feature. Indeed, that is what the term "single-lens reflex" stands for. And changing them is something you can do many times as Canon has over 50 lenses, from ones that give you the same perspective as a fish to ones that enable you to stand far away and yet catch the subject big enough to fill up an entire picture.

Words really can't express the excitement that is SLR photography. Being able to use an array of different lenses and accessories, the multitude of possibilities is truly mind-expanding. The pictures on the following pages just scratch the surface.

Here's a good way to make a faceless building come alive; a combination of architecture and sun.

A bird? A plane? No, it's a hang glider, taken with a long-distance (telephoto) lens.

Like something out of a science-fiction movie, the lights of the city seem to jump right out at you. Taken with a zoom lens.

With a long-range (telephoto) lens, the kids never suspected a thing. A good example of candid photography.

Breathtaking landscapes like this deserve to be preserved on film and observed time and again.

A pop-art painting? No, it's actually crystallized fixer used in photographic developing taken through a microscope at 60X.

Now you know how they make monster movies. Actually, it's just the head of a damsel fly, blown up five times its real size.

Another example of a still-life is the intricacies of a pocket watch's mechanism, close up.

Flowers are beautiful but when you magnify them as in this life-size picture of a poppy, they almost become extraterrestrial.

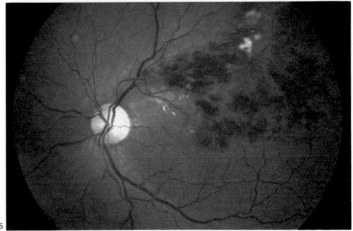

In another photographic realm, doctors often use pictures such as this of a diabetic's eye.

Part 2

Introduction to Canon A Series cameras;
The basic knowledge you need to get good
pictures effortlessly, and have fun doing
it; A detailed introduction to the AE-1 and
AV-1 cameras and the Canon photographic
system.

Even among SLR cameras, there is a wide variety you have to choose from. Still, all modern SLRs, regardless of the maker, have certain basic things in common. First, they all use the same type of film, 35mm, which can be bought any place film is sold. Next, they employ through-the-lens metering which means they have a built-in light meter that measures the light as it comes through the lens from the subject. Darkness and fast action are no obstacle with these cameras, either, as they can accept flash units and what are called power winders or motor drives. There's also one other condition a camera must fulfill to be a true SLR in the present-day sense: it must be complemented by a full range of accessories and interchangeable lenses.

Canon's SLRs, of course, offer all these things and even more. Four out of five of its A series cameras have the added advantage of automation. That is, all you basically have to do is set a control, focus and shoot to take a picture. There's the A-1, at once the most advanced, most feature-packed, most automatic and most professionally oriented of the four. It has a total of five automatic modes plus manual override. One of those modes truly lets you just focus and shoot. The A-1 also has a lot of other little features designed for the trickier photographic situations. Since this camera was designed with the professional in mind, however, there is one catch—it is expensive. The AE-1, AE-1 PROGRAM and AV-1 on the other hand, are probably within your budget and are easy to use as well.

As the first in Canon's automatic SLR line, the AE-1 was really a pioneer camera. It was the first to employ advanced electronics, in the form of a mini-computer called a CPU (central processing unit). This computer makes all exposure decisions leaving you with only the decision of whether or not to freeze the action, done by manipulating something called the shutter speed. Because you are free to decide that aspect of taking a picture, this kind of camera is known as shutter-speed priority (or shutter preferred). This mode is the mainstay of the AE-1 PROGRAM , too. And like the A-1, it also has a Programmed AE Mode which

sets both the aperture and the shutter speed automatically. The AV-1 is another Canon SLR which uses electronics but with it, you have to decide how much of the picture you want to be in focus; in other words, control the aperture. The advantages of both kinds of AE (automatic exposure) photography and the effects possible are described fully later on.

The last camera in the A series is the AT-1. With it, you have to control both of the just-mentioned things for proper exposure by matching two needles in the viewfinder. In spite of exposure not being automatic, however, the AT-1 also employs electronics. That's so it can use the five electronic Speedlite (flash) units and the Power Winder A for rapid, continuous film advance. These are handy accessories and one of the former is a must if you want to take pictures in the dark. And all can be used commonly on any camera in the series.

Regular, flash or continuous photography. Automatic's the name of the game with Canon's A series cameras. Now it's time to introduce what exactly the system has to offer.

It goes without saying that, when you buy a camera, the lens and film do not come with it. You have to purchase them separately. So don't be alarmed when you open the camera box and see only the body. There's nothing wrong. It's just that the lens is in another box. And the type of lens you should buy with your camera depends on several factors which are described later in this part. The same is true of film, which you can obtain at any camera store.

Besides the camera body, however, there are several other things that you will find in an AE-1 camera box. One is a battery to power the camera. Don't lose it as the camera will not work until a battery is inserted. You will also find several booklets. Don't throw them away as they are important. One is the owner's instruction manual which you should definitely read before trying to operate the camera. It provides valuable tips on taking pictures. The other booklet is about the Canon FD system of interchangeable lenses. You will also get a warranty card which you should fill out and send to Canon just in case a breakdown in your equip-

ment should occur. Read the booklet and you will be amazed at the variety of lenses Canon has to offer.

A few other accessories are also provided with your camera. There is the strap that enables you to carry the camera slung over your shoulder and an eyecup. The eyecup serves to block out light coming from the outside because your face can come right up to the camera. The scene you see in the viewfinder will thus appear even brighter than usual. A case for your camera may be included in the package as well, though it is sometimes sold separately. In either event, using one will protect your camera and help it stay like new.

The above things are true not only of the AE-1, but likewise for the other cameras in the A-series. It is now time to talk about these cameras.

Take a camera body out of its box and remove its body cap. You are now staring at a gaping hole inside of which is a mirror. But don't worry. The lens that you should have bought along with the camera will fit right in that hole. And with a slight turn, it will snap into place. At least, that's how it works with Canon's New FD lenses. Since they have to be automatic to match the automatic functions of the camera itself, every pin and lever on the bottom part of the lens finds its counterpart on the body. This perfect fit enables exact transmission of signals concerning exposure from the camera to the lens. And it's one reason why Canon's lenses are the best for Canon's cameras (other lens manufacturers make lenses that can be adapted to most types of SLR).

There are other reasons why Canon's lenses are the best for the job, too. Take the mount for instance. On many makers' lenses, the part where the signals and pins are located moves when the lens is mounted and dismounted. In this process, it rubs against its point of contact on the body, causing wear and an eventual deterioration in precision that is all important to an instrument like a camera. This part on Canon's breech-lock mount does not move, however, thus avoiding this problem (although the lens barrel rotates). Which is why Canon was able to put more signals and pins on its lenses, enabling such breakthroughs as shutter-speed priority on the AE-1 and five automatic modes on the A-1.

Canon has come up with other innovations for its lenses as well. Like a special focusing system for some telephoto lenses, specially designed glass and a multi-layer coating now applied to almost all lenses to give sharper images. Suffice it to say that, since a camera is nothing without a lens, a lot of energy has gone into perfecting the FD lens system. By the way, the proper name is the New FD Lens System. Yes, there is an old one. Its lenses were a bit bigger and were affixed to the camera by turning a chrome ring rather than the whole lens. The mount itself has not changed, however, so that even if you do get a hold of an older lens, it can be used. In fact, that's one of the unique things about the Canon photographic system: Both new and old lenses, even the non-automatic FL ones, can be used on any Canon camera past, present or future.

Any system's lenses come in all different shapes, sizes and focal lengths (the latter of which is engraved on the lens barrel). Generally speaking, the longer the focal length, the larger the lens. Perhaps you will see the logic in this when you realize that the focal length determines the size of the subject on the film. The longer the focal length, the bigger the image appears. Each lens also has its own angle of view, which determines how much is actually captured on film, or the sphere of your photography. The larger this angle becomes, the more of a scene that can be included in the picture.

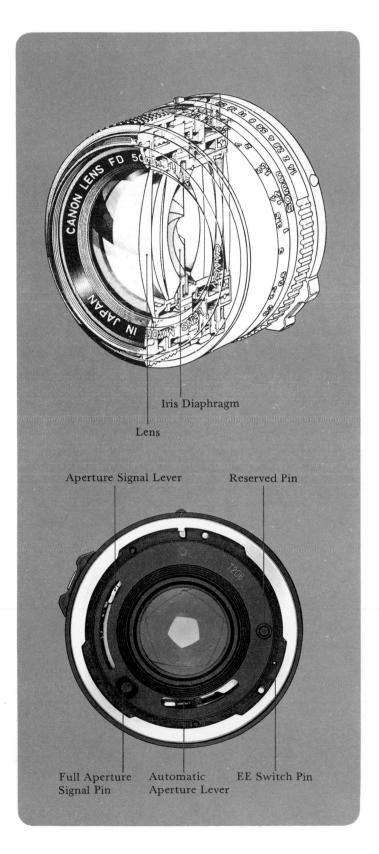

Iris Diaphragm

Lens

Aperture Signal Lever   Reserved Pin

Full Aperture Signal Pin   Automatic Aperture Lever   EE Switch Pin

7

The only reason for bringing up the boring subject of terminology is because, in talking about one's system it is quite common to hear, for example, "I have an AE-1 body with a 50 mm lens." This lens is considered by most people to be *the* standard lens, which is why it is the lens that is most often bought with a camera. But why is the 50 mm considered to be standard? Because the angle of view afforded by one of these lenses is the closest to that of the human eye.

Of course, you aren't limited to just a standard lens. Canon offers over fifty lenses, with focal lengths ranging from 7.5 mm to 1200 mm. With a choice like that, the discoveries that start with the first lens you buy for your SLR will never cease.

There is something in photography called the decisive moment. If you want to become a better-than-average picture-taker, you shouldn't let this moment slip by unnoticed. That's because it's the split second where action is at its climax, that one instant that gives a stupendous picture. Many times, to capture the decisive moment on film you have to be a virtual Wyatt Earp on the draw. But there are two devices that will make the job easy for you — the Power Winder A2 and A.

Slim, rectangular units they screw into the bottom of any A series camera and are a perfect fit. What they do is this: When you press the shutter button and hold it in while the Power Winder A2 or A is attached and turned on, in about 18 seconds a whole 36-exposure roll of film will be exposed. The built-in motor of these accessories (run by four penlight batteries) winds the film for you at about two frames per second, thus saving precious seconds that would normally be taken up by your thumb throwing the film advance lever. When it comes to fast, action-packed subjects whose decisive moments come and go in the twinkle of an eye, the Power Winder A2 or A is indispensable. They can automatically wind the film one frame at a time, too. This is convenient when you don't have a free hand to do it yourself or when the camera is resting on or against a stationary object for support and cannot be moved.

And in case you're wondering, exposure will be automatic since both these units connect with the camera's electronics. The same is true if you want to use a flash unit with the winder as well.

Sometimes, like when you want to take that picture of your kids indoors, there may not be enough light. You will have to allow light to strike the film for a much longer time by slowing down the shutter speed. But this is an operation fraught with the danger of camera movement. In other words, your pictures will come out blurred due to an imperceptible movement of your hands while the shutter is open. To eliminate this worry, you can use a flash unit to throw additional light onto your subject.

Canon has five such dedicated units for the A series cameras that slide right onto the top of the camera, into the hot shoe. Canon calls them Speedlites and they are the 133A, 155A, 177A, 188A and 199A. There are many, many different makes of flashes on the market

but the thing special about these particular ones is that they incorporate electronics just like those used in the camera. Therefore, they coordinate perfectly with the camera to ensure proper exposure.

Using them is simple as well. With the A-1 and AE-1 cameras, just turn the Speedlite on, wait for the pilot lamp to glow and press the shutter button. There's an intermediate step with the AV-1 and AT-1, which entails merely moving a ring on the lens. At any rate, these electronic gadgets are an incredible improvement over just a few years ago when flash photography necessitated calculations and lots of experience. It's just further proof of how simple photography in general has become.

Even this boy on the trampoline indoors is stopped in mid-flight and in perfect exposure with the Speedlite 155A.

To get fidgety children on film indoors, a flash is practically a must. Taken with Canon AE-1 and Speedlite 155A.

SPEEDLITE 199A

SPEEDLITE 177A

SPEEDLITE 155A

SPEEDLITE 133A

Even though these five Speedlites give basically the same effects, they are different power-wise. The 199A is the big gun; with it flash coverage up to 34.8ft. away is possible. The 188A and 177A are good up to 29ft. away, the 155A to 20ft. and the 133A to 13ft. (distances change according to ASA and auto aperture used). If, on the other hand, you're looking more for compactness, the latter two units would be the better choice. Then again, if you want special effects like softening the light thrown on your subject or making the background and foreground more in balance, the

199A's head tilts upward to three different positions and changeover to manual control is possible. In addition, while all these units are powerful enough to cover lenses as wide as 35mm, the 199A, 188A and 177A can accept a Wide Adapter accessory for coverage up to 24mm in the case of the 199A and 28mm for the latter two.

Sufficiently impressed with the selection of accessories Canon has to offer? This is only the tip of the iceberg.

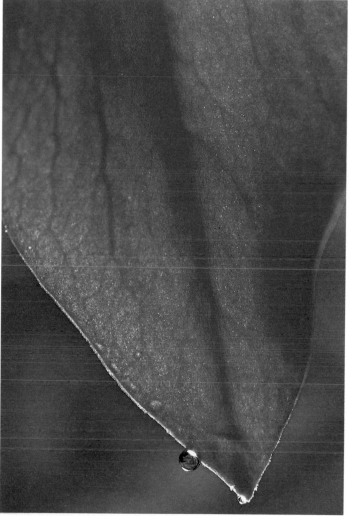

Some of the pictures in Part I were what is known as close-ups, or photomacrography. Here again is a world that used to be the domain solely of the professional. But you, with your automatic Canon and some of the accessories shown here, can easily experience this world. They range from the close-up lens that just screws right on to your regular lens to a fairly involved set-up with a microscope. In between is a whole bunch of lenses and attachments designed to get you closer to and more intimate with your subject. The photographer of the damsel fly in Part I probably didn't realize what that insect actually looked like until he viewed it through his photomacrographic equipment. Similar surprises will be in store for you as well, if and when you decide to try this kind of photography. In Canon's system, you'll find almost any piece of equipment your heart desires and your creativity demands.

The leaf from a Chinese Bellflower magnified two times. Equipment used were the AE-1, New Macro FD 50mm f/3.5, Bellows FL and a tripod.

More precise information about how to take this kind of picture can be found on pages 144—149.

❶ Handy Stand F
❷ Photomicro Unit F
❸ Attachment Rings
❹ Microphoto Hood
❺ Eyecup 4S
❻ Extension Tube M Set
❼ Lens Mount Converter A
❽ Macro Auto Ring
❾ Lens Mount Converter B
❿ Macrophoto Coupler FL 55mm
⑪ Slide Duplicator
⑫ Lens Hoods
⑬ Release 50
⑭ Release 30
⑮ Filters
⑯ Dioptric Adjustment Lenses S
⑰ Angle Finder A2
⑱ Angle Finder B
⑲ Magnifier S
⑳ Copy Stand 4
㉑ Duplicator 35
㉒ Auto Bellows
㉓ Roll Film Stage
㉔ Double Cable Release
㉕ Bellows FL
㉖ Bellows M
㉗ Macro Stage
㉘ Duplicator 8
㉙ Duplicator 16
㉚ New Macro FD 50mm f/3.5
㉛ New Macro FD 100mm f/4
㉜ Extension Tube FD 15-U
㉝ Extension Tube FD 25-U
㉞ Extension Tube FD 50-U
㉟ Macrophoto Lens 35mm f/2.8
㊱ Macrophoto Lens 20mm f/3.5
㊲ Close-up Lenses
㊳ AE-1 + Macrolite

Selecting the proper 35mm film is an important step towards getting good pictures, which is why it must be done with careful thought. To be taken into consideration are things like, "Will I be shooting outdoors or indoors? If outdoors, will it be a bright or cloudy day?"

The problem is that, if you use slide film, there are several types. Some are made specially for use indoors under tungsten lighting while others are for outdoor daylight conditions. If you would use, for example, daylight film indoors under incandescent lighting, your pictures will come out yellowish. On the other hand, using tungsten film outdoors gives a bluish tinge. Although this problem can be corrected by special filters (see pages 104–105), you should try to avoid the situation when buying your film.

If you are like the majority of photographers around the world, though, you will use regular print or negative film. Besides being easier to show than slides, prints are also free of the above indoor/outdoor problem. That's because they are made from negatives (which makes colors basically the reverse of what they are naturally). The negative enables the developers to correct any color discrepancies. Since slides lack this intermediate step, such correction is not possible. In spite of this disadvantage with slides, there is also an advantage: When the proper type of film is used, color rendition is gen-

Tungsten film used indoors under incandescent lighting

10

Daylight film used indoors under incandescent lighting

11

Daylight film used outdoors

12

Tungsten film used outdoors

13

erally better than with prints. Which is why most professionals use slide (also known as positive) film.

Measures of Film Sensitivity

ISO	6/9°	(8/10°)	(10/11°)	12/12°	(16/13°)	(20/14°)	25/15°	(32/16°)	(40/17°)	50/18°	(64/19°)
ASA	6	• (8)	• (10)	12	• (16)	• (20)	25	• (32)	• (40)	50	• (64)
DIN	9	• (10)	• (11)	12	• (13)	• (14)	15	• (16)	• (17)	18	• (19)

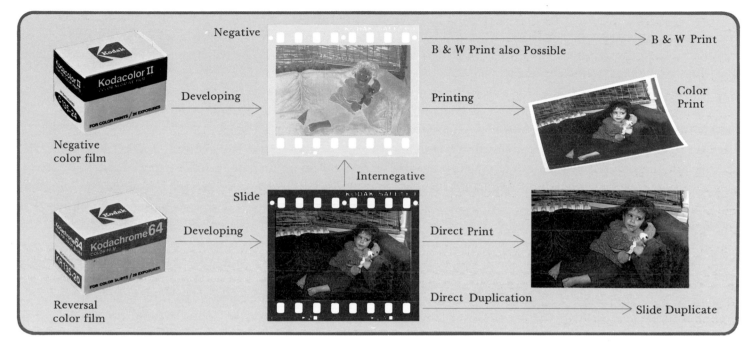

Perhaps even more important than the indoor/outdoor, slide/print decision, is what ASA to use. Although ASA is an acronym for the former American Standards Association, what it really refers to is a film's sensitivity to light. On any film box you will see ASA along with a number. The lower this number, the lower the film's sensitivity. So why not just use high-ASA film all the time? There are now very good ASA 400 films on the market that enable you to take great pictures in dim light or even in the dark. The trouble is, another characteristic of films is that they become less and less sharp the higher the ASA, making pictures taken with them appear grainy. So if sharpness and clarity are what you are after, and you have enough light, films within the ASA 25 to 32 range will give best results. Or you can avoid both extremes and choose a medium-speed film in the ASA 64 to 125 range.

And one last thing about film sensitivity. ASA is not the only standard used. DIN is used in many parts of Europe and there is now a new one called ISO that is being used internationally. You may find all three on your film box but with all of them, the higher the number, the higher the sensitivity.

The above discussion has centered around color film. But black and white film is also available, and in various sensitivities. Since it expresses everything in shades of white and gray, you may think this type of film is not very interesting. However, pictures taken in b&w are often highly effective and artistic. And you can have great control over the final prints by developing them yourself, a fairly easy process if you've got the basic equipment.

By the way, there are all sorts of film manufacturers, such as Kodak, Fuji, Fotomat and Ilford. You also have a choice of 12, 20, 24 or 36 exposures, depending on the film type.

(80/20°)	(100/21°)	(125/22°)	(160/23°)	200/24°	(250/25°)	(320/26°)	400/27°	(500/28°)	(640/29°)	800/30°	(1000/31°)	(1250/32°)	1600/33°	(2000/34°)	(2500/35°)	3200/36°	(4000/37°)	(5000/38°)	6400/39°	(8000/40°)	(10000/41°)	12800/42°
• (80)	100	• (125)	• (160)	200	• (250)	• (320)	400	• (500)	• (640)	800	• (1000)	• (1250)	1600	• (2000)	• (2500)	3200	• (4000)	• (5000)	6400	• (8000)	• (10000)	12800
• (20)	21	• (22)	• (23)	24	• (25)	• (26)	27	• (28)	• (29)	30	• (31)	• (32)	33	• (34)	• (35)	36	• (37)	• (38)	39	• (40)	• (41)	42

One thing that used to stand in the way of obtaining good photographs was exposure. Now this is no problem due to the automation of the A-series cameras. But what exactly does exposure mean?

Essentially, it is a combination of several things. One is film sensitivity (ASA) that the camera, after you have set it, automatically takes into account. The other factors are the amount of light that reaches the film and the length of time that light has to do its work. The mechanism that controls the former of these is called aperture, the latter shutter speed. On the AE-1 and AE-1 PROGRAM you set the shutter speed and the ASA (according to the film you are using) while the camera automatically selects the aperture for perfect exposure. With the AV-1, it's the other way around; you choose the aperture, the camera automatically sets the shutter speed.

Actually, you could set both yourself. Just think of the relationship between aperture and shutter speed in terms of doubles. One shutter speed faster means one aperture size larger. Likewise, one shutter speed slower requires the next smaller aperture. The chart on page 39 shows this relationship. (Their relationship with the ASA works on the same principle. Doubling ASA, say from 50 to 100, requires either increasing the shutter speed one step or decreasing the aperture size by one-half.)

This doesn't mean that you can first set the shutter speed or aperture anywhere you like, however. You have to find the right combination of the two to fit the amount of light coming from your subject. There is a simple way to express this brightness. Exposure value, or EV, is a number given to certain aperture/shutter speed combinations. Though this number changes with the ASA, the table on the next page uses ASA 100 as the standard. These numbers are based on a complex mathematical formula but all you need to know is that the higher the number, the brighter the condition. By looking at the EV table, you can see that there are several different combinations for one EV. If you select,

for instance, a shutter speed of 1/60 sec. under EV-2 conditions, underexposure will result as there is no aperture big enough to let the proper amount of light in.

Actually, the EV range can go all the way from −3 to 19; the closer you get to the extremities, the less the

To understand this concept better, take your camera outdoors and do a little experiment. Say, for example, you have the AE-1. Set it to any of the numbers on the shutter speed dial. Let's pick 125. Point the AE-1 at a fairly bright subject and note in the viewfinder the possible aperture/shutter speed combinations that will give proper exposure. Although modern automatic SLRs make discussion of this subject a bit passé, it would be helpful to keep EV numbers in mind if for no other reason than to understand camera specifications. The effective range of an exposure meter differs from camera brand to camera brand. The A-1, for example, can meter down to EV-2, good enough for metering a night sky slightly illuminated by surrounding lights. Of course, even if your camera can't meter down that far, you can still take the picture, by using a separate light meter or guesswork.

aperture that the camera chooses (by pressing the shutter button half-way). Now point the camera at a clear sky. See how the needle jumps upward to a smaller aperture? This is to compensate for the extra light by limiting the amount that reaches the film. If the sky is exceptionally bright, there may not be a small enough aperture to give correct exposure, which means the needle will end up in the red overexposure zone. In that case, you should choose a faster shutter speed.

Next, point the camera down to the ground. The aperture selected by the camera increases to allow more light to get to the film and thus enable correct exposure. If there isn't an aperture size big enough to give correct exposure, you will be duly warned in the viewfinder; slowing down the shutter speed will rectify the problem.

In this way you can also see the shutter speed/aperture relationship. Leave the camera aimed at the same subject and, while looking in the viewfinder, change the shutter speed one step in both directions. From 125, the next higher speed is 250 and the next lower is 60 since one speed is about double or half the next. The aperture the camera selects will then change automatically according to the new shutter speed. For instance, if the camera originally had selected f/5.6, it would change to f/4 at 250 and f/8 at 60. That's because, in spite of the numbers, f/4 is actually twice the size of f/5.6 and f/8 is half the size.

You can of course try this experiment with the AV-1, only everything is reversed. You set the aperture and watch the shutter speed that the camera selects change. And if you want to use the AV-1 like the AE-1, in other words shutter-speed priority, just set the aperture till the viewfinder shows the shutter speed you desire. Likewise, the AE-1 can be used like the AV-1 (aperture priority) by turning the Shutter Speed Dial till the viewfinder shows the aperture you want.

In addition, since a change in ASA will also make a difference in your exposure, you must not forget to set it on the camera. If you do forget, say, to turn the ASA dial from 100 to 400 when changing to ASA 400 film, a gap of two steps in exposure will occur (an increase of two EV).

EV Table [combination of aperture and shutter speed (sec)]

Shutter speed (sec) \ EV	18	17	16	15	14	13	12	11	10	9	8	7	6	5	4	3	2	1	0	-1	-2
30															22	16	11	8	5.6	4	2.8
15														22	16	11	8	5.6	4	2.8	2
8													22	16	11	8	5.6	4	2.8	2	1.4
4												22	16	11	8	5.6	4	2.8	2	1.4	
2											22	16	11	8	5.6	4	2.8	2	1.4		
1										22	16	11	8	5.6	4	2.8	2	1.4			
1/2									22	16	11	8	5.6	4	2.8	2	1.4				
1/4								22	16	11	8	5.6	4	2.8	2	1.4					
1/8							22	16	11	8	5.6	4	2.8	2	1.4						
1/15						22	16	11	8	5.6	4	2.8	2	1.4							
1/30					22	16	11	8	5.6	4	2.8	2	1.4								
1/60				22	16	11	8	5.6	4	2.8	2	1.4									
1/125			22	16	11	8	5.6	4	2.8	2	1.4										
1/250		22	16	11	8	5.6	4	2.8	2	1.4											
1/500	22	16	11	8	5.6	4	2.8	2	1.4												
1/1000	16	11	8	5.6	4	2.8	2	1.4													

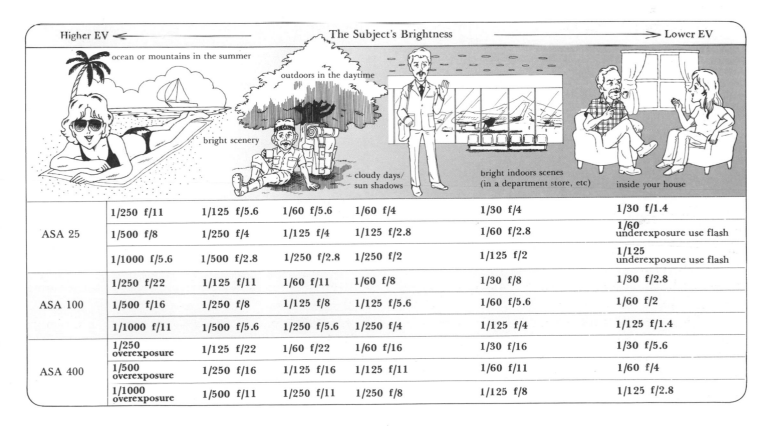

Higher EV ← The Subject's Brightness → Lower EV

ocean or mountains in the summer — outdoors in the daytime — bright scenery — cloudy days/sun shadows — bright indoors scenes (in a department store, etc) — inside your house

ASA 25	1/250 f/11	1/125 f/5.6	1/60 f/5.6	1/60 f/4	1/30 f/4	1/30 f/1.4
	1/500 f/8	1/250 f/4	1/125 f/4	1/125 f/2.8	1/60 f/2.8	1/60 underexposure use flash
	1/1000 f/5.6	1/500 f/2.8	1/250 f/2.8	1/250 f/2	1/125 f/2	1/125 underexposure use flash
ASA 100	1/250 f/22	1/125 f/11	1/60 f/11	1/60 f/8	1/30 f/8	1/30 f/2.8
	1/500 f/16	1/250 f/8	1/125 f/8	1/125 f/5.6	1/60 f/5.6	1/60 f/2
	1/1000 f/11	1/500 f/5.6	1/250 f/5.6	1/250 f/4	1/125 f/4	1/125 f/1.4
ASA 400	1/250 overexposure	1/125 f/22	1/60 f/22	1/60 f/16	1/30 f/16	1/30 f/5.6
	1/500 overexposure	1/250 f/16	1/125 f/16	1/125 f/11	1/60 f/11	1/60 f/4
	1/1000 overexposure	1/500 f/11	1/250 f/11	1/250 f/8	1/125 f/8	1/125 f/2.8

Some Shutter Speed Possibilities

B *BULB*

1 *ONE SECOND*

2 *HALF SECOND*

4 *FOURTH OF SECOND*

8 *EIGHTH OF SECOND*

15 *15th OF SECOND*

30 *30th OF SECOND*

60 *60th OF SECOND*

125 *125th OF SECOND*

250 *250th OF SECOND*

500 *500th OF SECOND*

1000 *1000th OF SECOND*

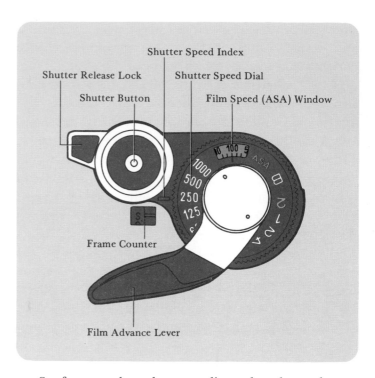

Shutter Speed Index

Shutter Release Lock

Shutter Speed Dial

Shutter Button

Film Speed (ASA) Window

Frame Counter

Film Advance Lever

So far, you have been reading a lot about shutter and shutter speed. But what exactly is a shutter? Actually, the dictionary defines it as, "Anything that covers an opening..." Such is it's function in a camera. It prevents light from striking the film until you want it to, and then controls the length of time the light has to do its work. It's a little like an eyelid; as long as the eyelid is open, light can enter the eye. But your eye

1/250 sec.

1/60 sec.

Here's a good example of how a fast shutter speed stops the action. Notice how blur-free it is!

This is the kind of picture you should avoid. Choose a faster shutter speed and everything will be OK.

doesn't have to worry about exposure, so it can stay open until it gets tired. Not so with film, though. If the shutter stays open too long, allowing too much light to strike the film, your picture will become overexposed, in other words, washed out. One way to prevent this, then, is to control the shutter.

Most SLR cameras have what is known as a shutter-speed dial. On it can usually be found numbers anywhere from 2000 to 1 and the letter B. 1 stands for 1 second, any number above that fractions of a second. Thus, 2 actually means the shutter will stay open for 1/2 sec.; 1000 means 1/1000 sec. With the Canon A-1, AE-1, AE-1 PROGRAM and AT-1 cameras, the choice of shutter speed is yours to make. There are some things to be careful of, however.

First of all, the slower the shutter speed, the more chance you have of getting a blurred subject. If the subject is moving and you use a slow shutter speed,

there will be enough time for the subject to move across the film. Indeed, when the picture is developed, that's what the subject will appear to be doing. Take a look at the pictures below. The left one was taken at 1/30 sec. Both the person and the car are in motion, though the stationary objects are not blurred. This is fine if your aim is to show motion but in this case it doesn't lend much to the picture. The second example was taken at 1/125. Motion of the person has been frozen, though the shutter speed still isn't fast enough to arrest that of the car. Two speeds faster at 1/500, however, succeeds. All sense of action has been removed and a better picture is the result.

The blur problem is compounded when using a telephoto lens as the picture is blown up larger than with a standard lens. Therefore, any slight camera movement will also be magnified. A shutter speed that is about the reciprocal of the focal length is recommended (1/250 sec. for a 300mm lens).

1/60 sec.
*With a 50mm lens,
it's nice and sharp.*

1/60 sec.
*With a 200mm lens,
it's hopeless without a tripod.*

1/30 sec.

1/125 sec.

1/500 sec.

By the way, it's not necessarily always true that a slow shutter speed will cause a moving subject to come out blurred. This phenomenon will definitely happen if your subject, as with the woman below, is moving parallel to the film. However, blurring decreases as the angle between the film and subject gets wider so that when the subject is coming directly at the camera, blur is hardly evident. This principle is illustrated pictorially below. Since a subject parallel to the film produces a whole exposure-worth of left-to-right movment, blur cannot be avoided. But the more the subject-to-film angle increases, the less the amount of film that gets covered with movement. Finally, only one spot on the film records movement, keeping blur to a minimum.

You will find that distance makes a difference in blur as well. If your subject is fairly far away, even a speed of 1/60 sec. will stop the action (though blur will probably be evident if the picture is enlarged). At close distances on the other hand, a 1/60 sec. shutter speed will yield blur because the subject's movement appears bigger on the film.

Another reason a subject, moving or not, may become blurred is camera movement. Of course, the camera doesn't actually move by itself. What's moving is your hand holding the camera. One way to prevent this is to hold the camera rock steady, with arms snugly up against your body. Then, you should also select a fast shutter speed. Again, 1/250 sec. or above is recommended.

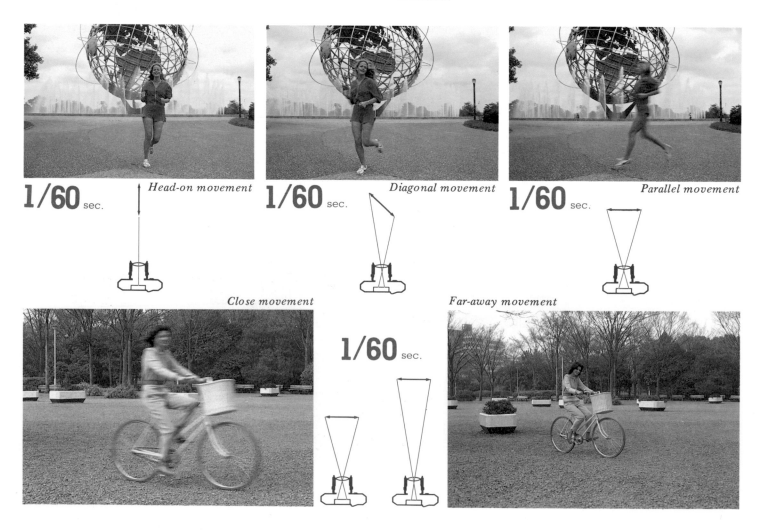

1/60 sec.   ↑ *Head-on movement*

1/60 sec.   *Diagonal movement*

1/60 sec.   *Parallel movement*

Close movement

1/60 sec.

Far-away movement

You may think that 1/125 or even 1/60 sec. is O.K., and for most situations, they seem to give acceptable sharpness. Sometimes, however, you may want to enlarge one of your favorite pictures. When doing that, even the slightest movement of your hand will show up in the enlargement, due to magnification. I think the six pictures on this page graphically illustrate this. Taken at 1/4, 1/15, 1/30, 1/60, 1/125, and 1/250 sec., you can see that the first two are total wipeouts. Succeeding ones are better, but if you look closely with a magnifying glass you'll see that the speck of white light on the lower right of the red part of the right eye doesn't really get sharp until the picture taken at 1/250 sec. Perhaps this is getting a bit picky. Indeed, one's idea of acceptable sharpness is largely a matter of individual taste. Use the shutter speeds that give you the results you want.

4
4th SECOND
Terrible blur!

15
15th SECOND
Not as bad but it still hurts.

30
30th SECOND
Not quite yet!

60
60th SECOND
Perhaps acceptable.

125
125th SECOND
O.K. unless it's enlarged.

250
250th SECOND
Totally blur-free!

Although blur is to be avoided in most cases, it can sometimes be an effective creative tool. You should keep your eyes open for situations like the one of the duck on this page, where the subject is basically motionless, yet a part of it is moving. A slow shutter speed here will capture the feeling of motion because the part moving will be blurred, yet the subject itself will still be sharp.

Panning is another way to get the feeling of action. You've probably heard this term before in relation to motion picture-taking. Basically, it refers to following the subject's movement by moving the camera. When you do this with an SLR, the background becomes a flow of movement and, as long as your focusing is good

An example of when a fast shutter speed of 1/500 will be advantageous.

14

and you have stayed with the subject, it will be reasonably sharp. And even if it's not, so what? Maybe a totally blurred image of, for example, a horse galloping through a field would have a better effect than a sharper one. Anyway, a slight turn of the shutter-speed dial on either the A-1, AE-1, AE-1 PROGRAM or AT-1 is all you need to get the effect you desire (AV-1 does not have such a dial but shutter speed can be controlled indirectly by the lens' aperture ring). The only thing you have to be careful of is not to choose a speed so slow that no one can tell what it is you're attempting to shoot. And don't just always try for this kind of picture. Stopping action produces stupendous results, too.

Slow shutter speeds have other uses as well. As mentioned before, when you want to take night pic-

For this picture, a medium shutter speed of 1/125 will suffice.

At 1/8 sec., the resulting blur is effective in showing action. 15

tures, Canon's Speedlite flash units are available. Sometimes, however, the natural light is best. This is especially true when there are colorful lights which a flash would make not so colorful. Like the pictures on this page. One is an illuminated water fountain. The movement of water has created a dazzling display of light streaks for this family, a very space-age effect.

Some interesting results can be obtained by pointing the camera up to the sky, too. Especially on occasions such as the 4th of July, a shutter speed of several seconds is needed to get your local fireworks display on film. Even better detail is obtainable by using a telephoto lens. Of course, since both the above exam-

ples were taken at night, such slow shutter speeds were necessary. Although shutter speeds slower than 1 or 2 seconds are usually not written on the camera's shutter speed dial (the A-1 being an exception; it has shutter speeds as slow as 30 seconds), they are possible by using the B (BULB) setting. Turn the dial to B and the shutter will remain open for as long as your finger presses the shutter button. How long should you keep it pressed down? Until the particular firework burst you want is over. Just make sure you don't leave the shutter open too long lest the surrounding light is picked up or your battery gets worn down. And with the B setting, since automatic exposure photography is not possible, you have to set the aperture yourself. f/5.6 for ASA 25, f/8 for ASA 64 and f/11 for ASA 100 is recommended but to make sure, try bracketing (taking the same picture at different exposures). Remember that the slightest hand movement causes blur. For these kinds of pictures, mounting the camera on a tripod, or bracing it against some stationary object, is a must. You can also use a special device, a cable release, in place of your finger to release the shutter.

This family's close encounter is actually only with an illuminated water fountain. Taken at a speed of 1/4 sec.

16

Leaving the shutter open for 4 or 5 seconds was long enough at f/11(ASA 100) to capture these fireworks in all their colorful splendor.

17

Have you ever looked at someone's eyes when bright light suddenly hits them? The pupils quickly become much smaller, a reaction that keeps too much light from entering the eye. In your camera, it's the diaphragm that closes down to limit the amount of light. If you point a camera at yourself, you can actually see this happening (though it's difficult with fast shutter speeds and big apertures). When you press the shutter button, several diaphragm blades move to form a hole called the aperture, the size of which either the camera or photographer has selected. After exposure, the blades return to their wide-open position, a condition known as full or maximum aperture. The size of the full aperture differs from lens to lens, a fact that has a lot to do with their cost; one with a larger aperture (also called f/stop or f/number) will cost more. By the way, the above operation of the diaphragm blades closing and opening is known as automatic diaphragm and is another modern improvement over cameras of old. It used to be that the blades would close down as soon as the photographer set the aperture, thus limiting the light that could reach the viewfinder. With the modern SLR, the blades don't close down until the picture is taken, enabling you to see the scene as you normally would and allowing you to change focus right up until the last moment. This system, full-aperture metering, also has a slight drawback, as explained on the next page.

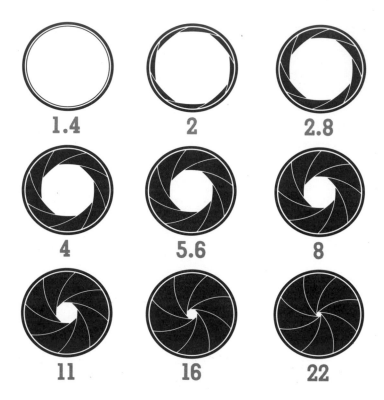

Now, let's talk about the aforementioned f/numbers. Although these numbers are written on the lens barrel thusly —1.4, 2, 2.8, 4, 5.6, 8, 11, 16, 22, 32— you will find them in print expressed as f/8, 1:8, F8, etc. These numbers are based on mathematical computations but what you need to know is this: Going upwards one step from any f/number means a one-half decrease in aperture size; going down will double the size. That is why when you change shutter speeds from, say, 125 to 250 (in effect halving the exposure), the aperture size will increase one f/number (f/8 to f/5.6 for instance) to give the same exposure. A quick look at this scale will also tell you how "fast" a lens is, in other words, the maximum aperture it possesses. Therefore, scales will differ slightly from lens to lens. In spite of that, an f/number on one lens will admit the same amount of light as the same number on a different one.

Control of the aperture means more than just adjusting light amounts. It also has a close relationship with something called depth of field. This refers to the

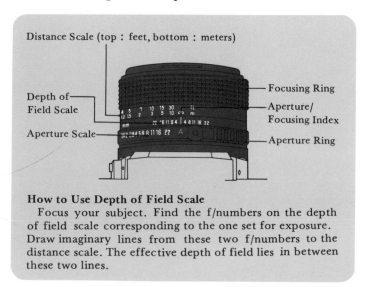

Distance Scale (top : feet, bottom : meters)

Depth of Field Scale

Aperture Scale

Focusing Ring

Aperture/ Focusing Index

Aperture Ring

How to Use Depth of Field Scale
Focus your subject. Find the f/numbers on the depth of field scale corresponding to the one set for exposure. Draw imaginary lines from these two f/numbers to the distance scale. The effective depth of field lies in between these two lines.

The combination of a 100mm lens and f/4 aperture produces this artistically blurred background.

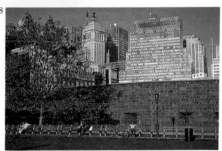

With a 50mm lens and aperture of f/16, this whole view of the Big Apple is in focus.

1.8

At f/1.8, you can see that the only thing in focus is the model.

5.6

This is a little better, but still none of the flags is in focus.

11

Now half the flags and the cars are sharp. But not the buildings.

22

Finally, at f/22, almost everything is in acceptable focus.

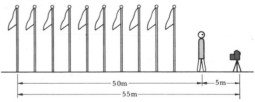

area in front and back of the subject that is in focus at the same time as your subject. Along with the kind of lens and position of the subject, the aperture you select has a definite bearing on whether the depth of field is great (a lot of the picture in focus) or shallow (only the subject and immediate area in focus). For instance, if you use an aperture of f/2, you may be surprised to find that although you have focused on the subject properly, not much else is very clear. That's because large aperture sizes equal shallow depth of field. If possible, changing to a smaller aperture and correspondingly slower shutter speed is advisable if you want some of the background in focus. You can also control depth of field by changing lenses and/or distance to the subject. Even with the same aperture and distance, the depth of field gets shallower the longer the focal length of the lens. With the same aperture and focal length, the depth of field gets shallower the closer you get to your subject.

There are several ways to tell what your depth of field is. Although full-aperture metering prohibits you from seeing this in the viewfinder normally, the A-1, AE-1, AE-1 PROGRAM and AT-1 come equipped with a stop-down lever. Push it in and, though the scene will become darker (because the lens is "stopped down" to

the aperture the camera or you have selected), you can tell precisely what will be in focus. This is an especially crucial step in close-up photography as the depth of field is usually so shallow. Another device you can use is the depth-of-field scale on the lens, as explained on the opposite page. At any rate, changing the aperture to control depth of field is a very important trick you can use to expand your photographic creativity.

The view through an AE-1 viewfinder. 1/250 sec. at f/5.6.

One thing in photography you can't afford to be soft on is focusing. Although there actually is a photographic effect known as "soft focus", it is different from "out-of-focus". The former eradicates harshness when taking shots of people. The latter is just plain bad photography.

Focusing is the one operation with the A series cameras where you are on your own. But it's an easy affair really, made even more so with a lot of help from a certain camera part—the viewfinder. As explained previously, an SLR's viewfinder, the place where you see the scene to be captured, receives the same light that goes through the lens for metering. Thus the viewfinder is, in most cases, quite bright since metering is done at full aperture.

The viewfinder also incorporates a focusing screen to help make the operation more accurate. Right in the middle is a split-image rangefinder, a horizontal line through a circle. If your subject is out of focus, the images in the top and bottom halves of the circle will not match. Just turn the focusing ring until they come together. And for even finer focusing adjustment, this circle is surrounded by a microprism ring that becomes cloudy when out of focus, clear when in.

With a fool-proof focusing system like this, you can't miss. Unless, that is, you have bad eyesight. If you do and find that your glasses are not strong enough or that they get in your way, Canon has a whole series of dioptric lenses available. Pick the one just right for you and slide it onto the eyepiece. You'll never need glasses for focusing again.

In focus. Strikingly sharp.

Out of focus. Fuzzy and unflattering.

A-1

Shutter Speed Readout   Aperture Readout

6 0   F   5 . 6   M

Flash Operation Signal   Manual Operation Signal

AE-1 PROGRAM

Manual Aperture "M" Signal

Programmed AE-Control LED

Aperture Scale

Stopped-down Metering Index Mark

Flash Charge-completion LED Display

AE-1

Overexposure Warning Mark

Manual Aperture "M" Signal

Battery Check and Stopped-down Metering Index Mark

Meter Needle

Aperture Scale

Underexposure/ Coupling Range Warning Lamp

AV-1

Overexposure Warning Index

Battery Check/ Camera Shake Warning Index

Shutter Speed Scale

Meter Needle

Underexposure Warning Index

AT-1

Battery Check/ Overexposure Warning Index Mark

Meter Needle

Aperture Needle

Underexposure Warning Index Mark

More than just a focusing aid, Canon camera viewfinders also function as a data bank. Using the AE-l as an example, it indicates to the right of the frame the aperture chosen by the camera (which gives you a hint about depth of field), tells you if the shutter speed you have set will cause overexposure and also indicates whether the battery has enough juice left or not. There are also two LED lamps, one that flashes when the camera is not on automatic, one that flashes if your exposure combination will lead to underexposure. You can glean all of this at one glance by just pushing down the shutter button half-way or pushing a special "Exposure Preview Switch" on the camera (to check the battery, a special switch is also provided). The A-1 and new AE-1 PROGRAM use LED's throughout for displaying information.

So far, we have discussed the basic things you need to know to control any SLR: shutter speed, aperture, ASA and focusing. The next section deals with actually using Canon equipment and the kind of system you should try to obtain.

Part 3

*Step-by-step instructions on how to use
the AE-1, AE-1PROGRAM, AV-1, Speedlites 188A and 177A; Introduction to
Canon's lens system and explanation of
angle of view and perspective; Group-by-
group discussion of Canon lens system
and description of recommended lenses;
When and how to use the Power Winder
A2.*

If you have bought a camera before, you undoubtedly noticed the accompanying instruction booklet. Many people tend to view it as a bother and throw it away, thinking the camera will be easy to operate. Of course, an SLR is easy to operate—once you've got the major steps down pat that is. Which is pretty hard without the instruction booklet.

Just in case you happen to be one of those people who threw away the booklet before realizing its importance, the following pages are provided as basic, step-by-step instructions on how to use the Canon AE-1, AE-1 PROGRAM and AV-1 cameras and Speedlites 188A, 177A.

Although Canon has five dedicated flashes for the A series of cameras—the 199A, 188A, 177A, 155A and 133A—the 188A and 177A are used here as examples. Regardless of which one you choose, the instructions for using all five are basically the same. Available for the professional photographer are two grip-type Speedlites, the 533G and 577G.

1 Set the Aperture Ring on the "A" Mark

First, attach the lens.
Remove the body and rear lens caps, align the red marks on the body and lens, turn the lens to the right until it stops.

When the lens is securely attached, the lens release button will pop out with a click.

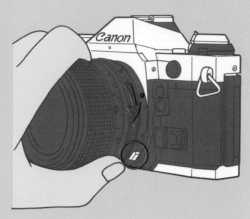

Turn the aperture ring to the "A" mark while pushing in the AE lock pin. The ring will become locked in this position.

Not doing so will make AE photography impossible.

2 Battery/Main Switch

Load the battery by inserting the lower (negative) end first and then pushing the upper (positive) end in. Make sure the poles are in the directions illustrated in the diagram inside the battery chamber.

The Main Switch has three settings: "A" for Advance, "L" for Lock and "S" for Self-timer. Turn the switch to "A" when you wish to take a picture. Make it a habit to keep it at "L" when not shooting, to avoid accidentally tripping the shutter.

If the battery is dead, the camera won't function. Check the battery condition by pressing the battery check button. If there is sufficient power, it will make a continuous, fast beeping sound.

3 Set the ASA

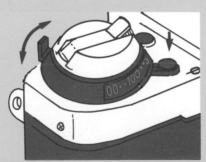

Press the lock release button beside the film rewind knob and slide the ASA setting lever until the number corresponding to your film's ASA appears in the window, aligned with the index.

Loading the Film

Pull the rewind crank up to open the back cover. Place the film cartridge into the film chamber as shown, making sure the glossy side is up.

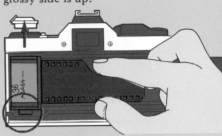

Pull the film across the camera and insert the end into any slot on the take-up spool.

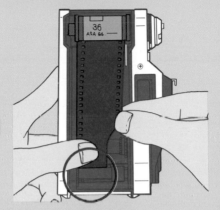

Throw the lever slowly to advance the film once. Check to see the film perforations are engaged in the teeth of the film transport socket and take-up spool.

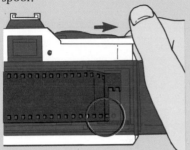

 Select the Exposure Mode

Programmed AE

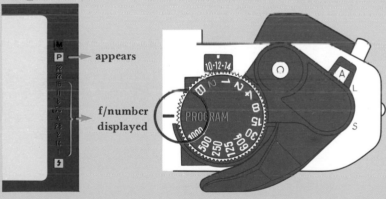

appears

f/number displayed

With Programmed AE, the camera sets both the shutter speed and aperture automatically. Turn the shutter speed selector dial to PROGRAM, confirming first that the lens is on "A".

Look into the viewfinder and press the shutter button half-way. On Programmed AE mode, a green P will appear, together with the f/number the camera has selected. The f/number is also displayed with shutter speed priority mode.

Shutter speed Priority AE

f/number displayed

The ideal mode for action photography. Turn the shutter speed selector dial until your desired shutter speed is aligned with the index mark.

As a guide, use this chart to choose the most suitable shutter speed.

| 60 | 125–250 | 500–1000 |

Viewfinder Warning Symbols

MODE / Lighting situation \ LENS	Programmed AE		Shutter Speed Priority		Bulb	
	A	M	A	M	A	M
Normal	AV　P	AV　M	AV	AV　M		M
Camera shake warning	AV　⊒P⊑	AV　M	AV	AV　M		M
Underexposure warning	⊒AVo⊑ ⊒P⊑₁	⊒AVo⊑　M ₂	⊒AVo⊑　2	⊒AVo⊑　M ₂		M
Overexposure warning	⊒16⊑　P	⊒16⊑　M	⊒32⊑	⊒32⊑　M		M
Auto-exposure flash	AVef　⚡	AVef　⚡M	AVef　⚡	AVef　⚡M	AVef　⚡	AVef　⚡M
Manual mode flash	⊒32⊑　⚡	⚡　M	⊒32⊑　⚡	⚡M	⊒32⊑　⚡	⚡M

A variety of information is displayed in the viewfinder to keep you informed of the exposure situation. The above chart shows what symbols appear and when. Key: A: Auto; M: Manual; P: Programmed AE; AV: Aperture value; AVo: Maximum aperture; AVef: Auto-flash aperture value; ⚡: Flash charge completed; ⊒⊑: Auto check indication.

Notes:　1) Flashes on and off when the auto-exposure runs out of both shutter speed and lens opening.
　　　　2) Flashes on and off when the auto-exposure runs out of lens opening.

✳ AE Lock

Firmly holding the camera, turn the focusing ring until your subject is clearest and gently press the shutter button all the way down.

AE Lock Operation

A strongly back-lit subject will come out under-exposed unless you compensate by widening the aperture. This is a simple task using the AE Lock switch, conveniently located by the lens. Move close in to your subject and press the shutter button halfway. Check the f/stop in the viewfinder and press in the AE Lock switch. Remove your finger from the switch but keep the shutter button depressed. Compose your picture (re-focusing if necessary) and press the shutter button all the way to take the picture.

Note how the model's face appears dark and almost in shadow. The background is nicely exposed but this isn't what's important.

Take a reading as close up to her face as possible and retain this reading with the AE Lock. Be careful, though, not to affect the reading with your own shadow.

There is always the chance of camera movement at speeds of 1/30 sec. or below with hand-held photography.

Subject under-exposed

Correctly exposed

6 Rewind the Film

Once all the pictures have been taken, press in the rewind button. (You can tell you're at the end because the film advance lever will not turn all the way, if at all. Do not force it!)

Unfold the rewind crank and turn in the direction of the arrow until the frame counter shows "S".

Open the back cover and remove the film cartridge.

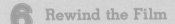

Pre-shooting Checklist

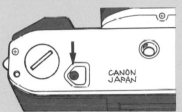

Is the aperture ring on the "A" mark?

Is the main switch at "A"?

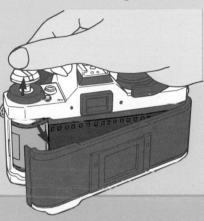

Is the film being advanced correctly?

Is there enough battery power?

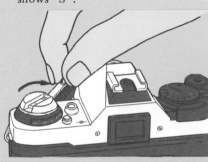

OR

Is the ASA set correctly?

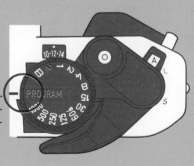

Is the shutter speed selector dial set to PROGRAM (for Programmed AE)?

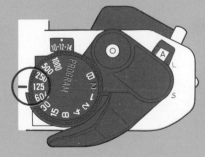

Is the shutter speed selector dial set to a suitable shutter speed (for shutter speed priority AE)?

Load four new AA size batteries taking care to observe the polarities indicated by the diagram on the bottom of the unit. Attach the cover, turning the screw with a coin.

Making sure the power winder's main switch is "OFF", remove the camera's winder coupler cover. Clean the winder's and camera's terminals with a soft cloth to ensure proper contact. Then securely attach the power winder to the camera by turning the fastening screw clockwise with a coin.

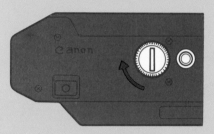

Set the power winder's main switch to "S" for single frame shooting or "C" for continuous. At the film end the red LED by the switch will light. Turn off the main switch and rewind the film. Failure to turn the switch off will deplete the power. When the switch is at "OFF" the film can be advanced manually with the film advance lever. Turn the power winder off whenever you are not using it.

After loading its four penlight batteries, slide the unit all the way into the accessory shoe from the back and tighten the screw at the base.

Leave the lens' aperture ring on the "A" mark.

Except for B, the shutter-speed selector dial can be set anywhere.

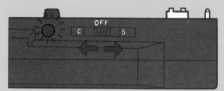

When using a Canon A series Speedlite on the AE-1 PROGRAM, both the aperture and shutter speed will be automatically set for correct exposure as soon as the pilot lamp comes on.

On the back of the Speedlite, set the ASA to match that set on the camera.

Set the aperture selection switch to the upper or middle position to select the auto shooting distance range (indicated by red and green lines, respectively.)

When the pilot lamp lights up after the unit has been turned on, you are ready to shoot.

A ⚡ symbol will appear in the viewfinder when the Speedlite is ready. After you take the picture it will blink on and off to confirm correct exposure.

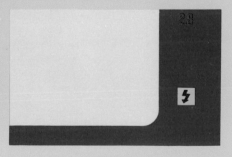

1. Shutter Speed/Program Mode Index
2. Shutter Speed Selector Dial Guard
3. Programmed AE Index
4. Shutter Speed Selector Dial
5. Film Advance Lever
6. Finger Rest
7. Main Switch
8. Shutter Release Button (with Cable Release Socket)
9. Frame Counter
10. Eyepiece
11. Automatic Flash Contacts
12. Flash sync. Contact
13. Film Plane Indicator
14. ASA Film Speed Setting Lever
15. ASA Film Speed Window
16. Film Rewind Knob with Crank
17. Battery Check Button
18. AE Lock Pin
19. "A" Mark
20. Aperture Ring
21. Distance Index
22. Focusing Ring
23. Action Grip
24. Battery Chamber Cover
25. PC Socket
26. AE Lock Switch
27. Exposure Preview Switch
28. Stop-down Lever
29. Lens Release Button
30. Tripod Socket
31. Winder and Motor Drive Coupler Cover
32. Film Rewind Button
33. Positioning Hole for Winder and Motor Drive
34. Terminals for Winder and Motor Drive
35. Memo Holder

Programmed AE with New FD 35–70mm f/2.8–3.5.

Programmed AE

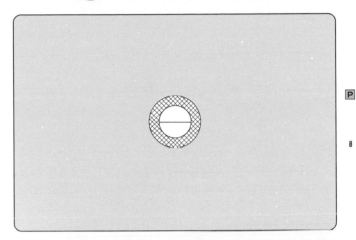

On programmed AE both the shutter speed and aperture are set automatically according to the brightness of the subject.

The above chart shows the programmed combinations of shutter speed and aperture. Thus, with ASA 100 film, when f/4 appears in the viewfinder the shutter speed will be 1/60 sec. Similarly, at f/8, the shutter speed will be 1/250.

Easy though Canon SLRs are to use, there are times when you want to be able to devote all your attention to the subject you are shooting. In such a case, you don't even want to have to adjust the shutter speed, necessary with shutter speed priority AE. The Canon AE-1 PROGRAM (like the A-1) has a mode which automatically sets both the shutter speed and the aperture—and leaves you to concentrate on catching the picture of a lifetime.

With Programmed AE, the camera uses its built-in electronic "brain" to choose the most suitable shutter speed and aperture. And it'll instantly change its mind if a change in the lighting situation warrants it. This can happen if say, your subject moves from an extremely bright, sunny spot into shadow.

Turn the shutter speed selector dial to "PRO—GRAM," checking first that the lens' aperture ring is on "A". A green P will appear when you depress the shutter release button half-way or press the exposure preview switch. All that remains for you to do is focus and shoot.

This same P will blink in warning in low-light situations. Make sure to hold the camera extra steady. Although the aperture is selected for you automatically the f/number will still appear in clear, red LEDs in the viewfinder, providing a guide to the depth of field.

Programmed AE and the New FD 70—210mm f/4 zoom.

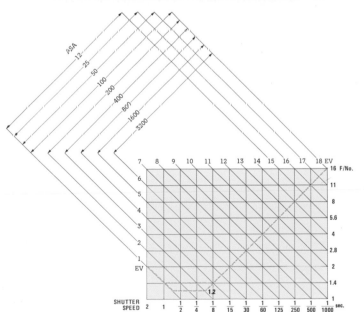

Shutter Speed Priority AE with New FD 35–70mm f/2.8–3.5, 1/8 sec.

Shutter Speed Priority AE

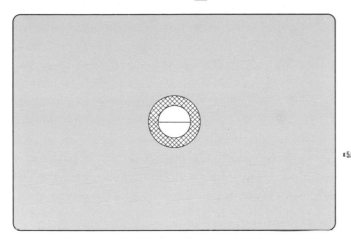

A 1/500 sec. shutter speed froze these seagulls in mid-air. New FD 400mm f/4.5 lens.

A rapid action scene can take place and become history in the blink of an eyelid. Which is why it is essential to use a fast shutter speed when photographing fast-moving subjects.

That basically is the reason why Canon several years ago decided to adopt the shutter speed priority format over the aperture priority system for most of its cameras. Shutter speed priority means that you set the shutter speed manually and the camera automatically chooses the right aperture according to the brightness of the scene. It's the other way around with aperture-priority. You set the aperture and the camera selects a shutter speed—which may be too slow if your aperture is too small.

The AE-1 PROGRAM's shutter speeds go as fast as 1/1000—which is fast enough to "freeze" even the speediest of subjects. On the other hand you can achieve equally dramatic effects by purposely blurring a moving subject to give the impression of speed. This is done by selecting a slower shutter speed.

For shutter-speed priority AE, turn the shutter-speed selector dial to your desired shutter speed. Make sure that the lens' aperture ring is on "A". Depress the shutter button half-way and the f/number chosen by the camera will be displayed, providing a handy reference to the depth of field. In case the f/number is outside the shutter speed's range, it will flash to warn you that the picture will be under- or over-exposed.

FOCUSING SCREENS

The focusing-screen—that all-important little optical plate which helps ensure exact focusing—is interchangeable on the AE-1 PROGRAM. There are no less than eight to choose from, including the standard New Split/Microprism screen, to suit the type of lens you intend to use or the characteristics of the subject. One screen features horizontal and vertical reference lines for architectural or copying applications, another has vertical/horizontal scales in millimeters for close-ups, photomacrography, etc., and yet another employs a unique system whereby the image is separated in four directions for focusing subjects predominantly made up of straight or curved lines and angles. The screen is installed in the mirror box. Use the special tool provided with the screen and take special care not to touch the screen's surface with your fingers, or the mirror.

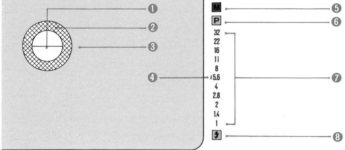

❶ New Split Rangefinder
❷ Microprism Ring
❸ Laser-matte Screen
❹ Stopped-down Metering Index Mark
❺ Manual Aperture Control LED
❻ Programmed AE Control LED
❼ Aperture Display
❽ Flash Charge-completion LED Display
   (with Speedlite 188A: AE Flash Confirmation Signal)

1. New Split/Microprism: Standard screen in the AE-1 PROGRAM. For general photography using any type of lens. Rangefinder does not black out, unlike the conventional rangefinder which blackens out at f/5.6.

2. Microprism: Matte/Fresnel field with microprism rangefinder in the center. Suited for general photography when using an aperture of f/5.6 or faster.

3. New Split: Matte/Fresnel field with split-image rangefinder in the center. Suited for general photography and can be used with small maximum aperture lenses.

4. All Matte: Matte/Fresnel field with clear matte center spot. Recommended for macro and telephoto photography where undistracted viewing of entire field of view is desired.

5. Matte/Section: Similar to (4) screen, but with horizontal and vertical reference lines. Recommended for architectural photography and copy work.

6. Matte/Scale: Matte/Fresnel field with clear matte center plus horizontal and vertical scales in mm's. Recommended for copy work and architectural photography where it is useful to know subject size.

7. Double Cross-hair Reticle: Matte/Fresnel field with 5mm clear center spot containing double cross-hair reticle. Recommended for photomicrography and astrophotography.

8. Cross Split-image: Matte/Fresnel field with cross split-image rangefinder in the center. Suited for general photography using fast lenses.

SPEEDLITE 188A

To take full advantage of the AE-1 PROGRAM's advanced electronics, Canon has brought out a new Speedlite. The 188A makes taking perfect automatic flash pictures easier than ever. All flash exposure information is shown in the viewfinder—so you never have to miss any of the action in order to check the flash. Turn the unit on and after a few seconds a green 🔓 will appear to tell you that all is ready. After you take your picture the 🔓 will flash, confirming that the exposure was correct. The camera automatically sets the 1/60 sec. flash sync. speed and selects the aperture as well.

The 188A has two auto apertures, besides manual: f/2.8 and f/5.6 with ASA 100 film, which correspond to distances of 1—9m and 0.5—4m respectively. Compact and light, it operates on four AA size batteries.

A wide adapter (standard accessory) enables flash coverage with lenses as wide as 28mm.

FLASH MODE	A-1	AE-1 PROGRAM	AE-1	AV-1	FUNCTIONS	
					Shutter Speed	Aperture
Full Auto Flash Mode	◎	◎	◎	—	Automatic Setting	Automatic Setting
Manual Flash	○	○	○	○	Automatic Setting	Manual Setting

◎: Normal method of use   ○: Usable

New FD 50mm f/1.8, f/5.6 auto flash aperture.

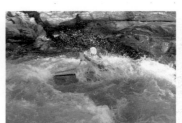

This action-packed series of shots tells a dramatic story. Power Winder A2 with New FD 35—70mm f/2.8—3.5 at 1/250 sec., AE.

POWER WINDER A2

Rapid-fire shooting is the principal advantage of the Power Winder A2. It advances the film at a brisk 2 frames per second and has a convenient switch for continuous/single-frame shooting. But there are other less obvious advantages which you will really appreciate once you have begun using it.

Take for instance close-up and macrophotography. Setting up your equipment and subject is a time-consuming business. You don't want to run the risk of jarring the camera and upsetting the picture composition by winding the film on manually. The Power Winder A2 is a friend indeed here. And with the A2 connected to your camera, you can even operate it by remote control from up to 60 meters away (under normal conditions). The box of tricks which lets you do this is the Wireless Controller LC-1. Using a tripod, set your camera by a river or lake and conceal yourself far enough away. The stunning pictures of wildlife you get will make everyone exclaim "How did you do it?"

It required the Motor Drive MA's rapid-fire capability to get this aspiring Evel Knievel on film. New FD 35mm f/2 at 1/125 sec., AE.

MOTOR DRIVE MA

Speed is of the essence if you want to catch the action at its most exciting. The ideal tool for this is the Motor Drive MA.

The Motor Drive MA's maximum 4 frames/sec film advance is fast enough to ensure that you'll never miss a perfect picture-taking opportunity again. Another setting winds the film at 3 fps and it can also be set for single-frame shooting.

The unit is easily attached to the body of the AE-1 PROGRAM. Light and compact, it forms a well-balanced match with the camera. Two power sources are available: the Battery Pack MA and the rechargeable Ni-Cd Pack MA. The Motor Drive MA can also be used with the Wireless Controller LC-1 for remote-control shooting.

Whether it's the thrills and spills of a football game or the Indy 500 or just for taking sequential shots of the goings-on at a child's birthday party, you'll find the Motor Drive MA is a great way to keep up with the action.

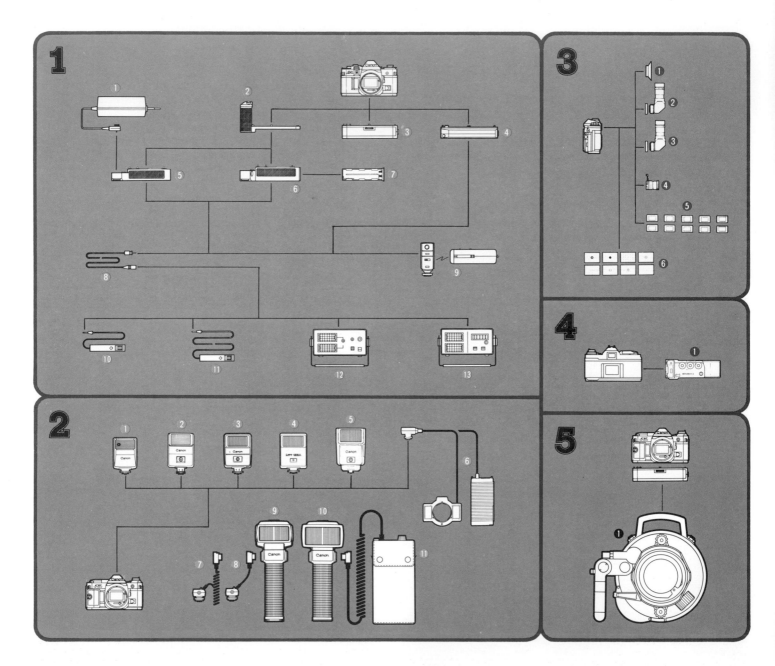

1 **Motorized Film Drive and Unmanned Photography**
① Ni-Cd Charger MA
② Motor Drive MA
③ Power Winder A
④ Power Winder A2
⑤ Ni-Cd Pack MA
⑥ Battery Pack MA
⑦ Battery Magazine MA
⑧ Extension Cord E 1000
⑨ Wireless Controller LC-1
⑩ Remote Switch 60
⑪ Remote Switch 3
⑫ Time Lapse Programmer, A Unit
⑬ Time Lapse Programmer, B Unit

2 **Flash Photography**
① Speedlite 133A
② Speedlite 155A
③ Speedlite 177A
④ Speedlite 188A
⑤ Speedlite 199A
⑥ Macrolite ML-1
⑦ Sensor Unit G100
⑧ Sensor Unit G20
⑨ Speedlite 533G
⑩ Speedlite 577G
⑪ Transistor Pack G

3 **Viewfinder System**
① Eyecup 4S
② Angle Finder A2
③ Angle Finder B
④ Magnifier S
⑤ Dioptric Adjustment Lenses S
⑥ Focusing Screens

4 **Date Imprinting System**
① Data Back A

5 **Underwater Photography**
① Marine Capsule A

CANON AE-1 PROGRAM

Type: 35mm single-lens reflex (SLR) camera with electronically controlled Automatic Exposure (AE) and focal-plane shutter.
Exposure Modes: Programmed AE, shutter speed priority AE, AE flash photography with specified Canon Speedlites, and manual override.
Format: 24 x 36mm
Usable Lenses: Canon FD (for full-aperture metering) and Canon FL and non-FD (for stopped-down metering) series lenses.
Standard Lenses: FD 50mm f/1.2, FD 50mm f/1.4, FD 50mm f/1.8
Lens Mount: Canon breech-lock mount.
Viewfinder: Fixed eye-level pentaprism. Gives 94% vertical and 94% horizontal coverage of the actual picture area with 0.83X magnification at infinity with a standard lens. Information is displayed in form of LED digital display to the right of field of view. Includes "P" mark (programmed AE and camera shake warning), "M" mark (manual aperture control indicator), aperture display (appropriate aperture flashes to warn of overexposure and underexposure), stopped-down metering index, "⚡" mark (flash charge-completion indicator with specified Canon flash units and auto flash confirmation signal with Speedlite 188A).
Dioptric Adjustment: Built-in eyepiece is adjusted to standard −1.0 diopter.
Focusing Screen: Standard split-image/microprism rangefinder and seven other types of interchangeable screens are optionally available.
Light Metering System: Through-the-lens (TTL), Central Emphasis Averaging System by SPC (Silicon Photo Cell).
Meter Coupling Range: EV 1 (1 sec. at f/1.4) to EV 18 (1/1000 sec. at f/16) with ASA/ISO 100 film and f/1.4 speed lens.
ASA Film Speed Scale: ASA/ISO 12 to 3200.
Exposure Memory: EV locked in when shutter release button is pressed halfway and the AE lock switch is pressed once. Exposure memorized as long as shutter button is pressed halfway.
Exposure Preview: By pressing shutter button or exposure preview switch.
Shutter: Cloth, focal-plane, 4-spindle, electronically-controlled. With shock and noise absorbers.
Main Switch: Three positions: "A," "L," and "S." At "L" all active circuits are cut off as a safety feature. "S" position is for self-timer photography.
Shutter Release Button: Two-step, electromagnetic with lock, cable release socket, and finger rest.
Shutter Speed Selector Dial: 2 sec. − 1/1000 sec., "B," and "PROGRAM" (for programmed AE). With guard.
Self-timer: Electronically-controlled. Main switch is set to "S." Activated by pressing shutter button. Ten-second delay with electronic "beep-beep" sound. Cancellation possible.
Stop-down Lever: For depth-of-field preview (FD lens) or metering (non-FD lens or close-up accessories).
Power Source: One 6V alkaline-manganese (Eveready [UCAR] No.537), 6.2V silver oxide (Eveready [UCAR] No. 544, JIS 4G13, Mallory PX28.), or lithium (Mallory PX 28L) battery. Battery lasts about one year under normal use.
Battery Check: "Beep-beep" sound when pressing battery check button. Number of beeps per second emitted decreases with power level.
Flash Synchronization: X synchronization at 1/60 sec.; M synchronization at 1/30 sec. or slower. Direct contact at accessory shoe for hot-shoe flash. PC socket (JIS-B type) with shock-preventive rim for cord-type

flash on front of body.
Automatic Flash: Full AE flash photography with specified Canon Speedlites. Shutter speed automatically set. Aperture automatically controlled according to setting of flash when pilot lamp illuminates.
Back Cover: Opened with rewind knob. Removable. With memo holder.
Film Advance Lever: Single-stroke 120° throw with 30° stand-off. Ratchet winding possible.
Film Counter: Additive type. Automatically resets to "S" upon opening back cover. Counts backwards as film is rewound.
Other Safety Devices: Camera will not function when power level insufficient. Film winding impossible while shutter is in operation.
Dimensions: 141mm x 88mm x 47.5mm (5-9/16" x 3-7/16" x 1-7/8") body only.
Weight: 575g (20-5/16 ozs.) body only.
745g (26-1/4 ozs.) with FD 50mm f/1.8 lens.

Power Winder A2 ...Usable for: A Series Cameras

Winding speed: Approximately 0.5 seconds. **Operation:** When the shutter release button on the camera is pressed, the winder will function. **Shutter Speed Coupling Range:** 1/60 to 1/1000 second for continuous photography. "B", or any shutter speed for single frame photography. (However, if set at "B", AE photography cannot be performed.) **Two Positions:** "C" for continuous shooting at about two frames per second. "S" for single frame shooting. **Automatic Cut-off Circuit:** When the film is completely wound or if the batteries become exhausted, the winder will automatically stop and the warning lamp (LED) will light up. **Power Source:** Four AA size 1.5V alkaline, carbon-zinc or Ni-Cd batteries. **Mounting on Camera:** By using tripod socket on the camera. **Size:** 140.8 x 53.4 x 27.5 mm (5-9/16" x 2-1/8" x 1-1/16") **Weight:** 275 g (9-11/16 ozs.) including batteries.

Speedlite 188A ...Usable for: A Series Cameras

Type: Electronic computer flash unit with series control system. **Guide Number:** 25 (ASA 100, m) or 41 (ASA 25, ft.). 16 (ASA 100, m) or 26 (ASA 25, ft.) with Wide Adapter 188A. **Recycling Time:** Less than 8 sec. using alkaline-manganese batteries. Less than 6 sec. using Ni-Cd batteries. **Number of Flashes:** About 200 using alkaline-manganese batteries. About 70 using Ni-Cd batteries. **Flash Coverage Angle:** Covers a 35mm lens. Covers a 28mm lens when Wide Adapter 188A is used. **Flash Duration:** 1/700 sec. to 1/50,000 sec. **Aperture/MANU Selection Switch:** Three positions: f/2.8 (red), f/5.6 (green), and manual (M) at ASA 100. **Auto Shooting Distance Range:** 1.0 to 9.0m (1.0 to 5.6m with Wide Adapter 188A) at red position. 0.5 to 4.5m (0.5 to 2.8m with Wide Adapter 188A) at green position. **ASA Film Speed Scale:** ASA 25 to ASA 800. **Aperture Scale:** f/1.4 to f/16. **Power Source:** Four penlight (AA) alkaline-manganese (AM-3, LR6) or Ni-Cd batteries. **Pilot Lamp:** Comes on when unit sufficiently charged. Also functions as flash test button. **Dimensions:** 68 (W) x 52 (D) x 103 (H)mm (2-11/16" x 2-1/16" x 4-1/16") **Weight:** 290g (10-1/4 ozs.) including batteries. **Accessories:** Soft Case, Wide Adapter 188A.

1 Set the Aperture Ring on the "A" Mark

First, attach the lens.

Remove the body and rear lens caps, align the red marks on the body and lens, turn the lens to the right until it stops.

When the lens has been completely attached, the lens release button will pop out with a click.

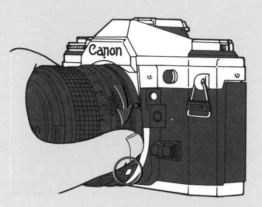

Turn the aperture ring to the Ⓐ mark while pushing in the EE lock pin. The ring will become locked in this position.

Not doing so will make AE photography impossible.

2 Insert the Battery

Open the battery chamber cover. Using the viewfinder cover taken from the accessory shoe or a fingernail is convenient for this purpose.

Load the battery by inserting the lower (negative) end first and then pushing the upper (positive) end in. Make sure the poles are in the directions illustrated in the diagram inside the battery chamber.

Do not touch the poles with your fingers.

(Suggestion: always clean both ends of the battery before putting it in the camera.)

3 Check the Battery (if battery runs out of power, the camera won't operate)

Press the battery check button while looking through the viewfinder.

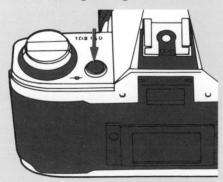

If there is enough power, the meter needle will rest at or below the battery check index. If it rests above the index or fails to come to rest after about 3 seconds, there's not enough juice.

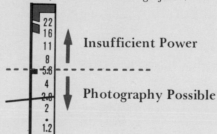

22
16
11
8
5.6   **Insufficient Power**
4
2.8   **Photography Possible**
2
1.2

A battery's performance declines in cold weather. Under such conditions, keep it warm near your body until you need to use it.

Set the ASA

Lift the knurled ring around the shutter speed dial, and turn until the number corresponding to that of the ASA written on the film box appears in the window, aligned with the index.

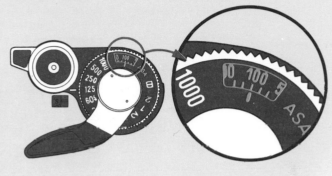

Load the Film

When loading outdoors, avoid direct sunlight. Making a shadow with your body is one way.

Pull the rewind crank up to open the back cover. Place the film cartridge into the film chamber as shown, making sure the glossy side is up.

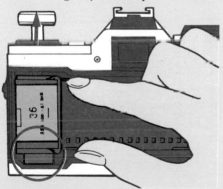

Pull the film across the camera and insert the end into any slot on the take-up spool.

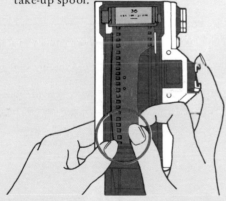

Throw the lever slowly to advance the film once. Check to see the film perforations are engaged in the teeth of the film transport sprocket and take-up spool.

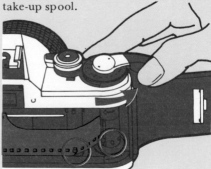

Make sure the film is taut before closing the back cover.

By repeatedly pressing the shutter button and throwing the film advance lever, advance the film to the first frame.

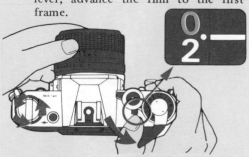

Everything is OK if the rewind crank rotates as the film advance lever is thrown.

6 Set the Shutter Speed

As a guide, refer to this chart to choose the most suitable shutter speed.

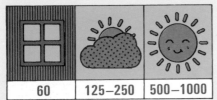

| 60 | 125–250 | 500–1000 |

Set the shutter speed you have decided on by turning the shutter speed dial until the corresponding number is aligned with the index.

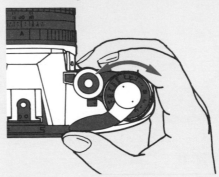

Look into the viewfinder and press the shutter button half-way. Check to make sure exposure is correct by looking at the meter needle.

If the meter needle moves into the red overexposure warning zone, select a faster shutter speed.

Correct Exposure

If the underexposure warning lamp starts to flash, choose a slower shutter speed.

7 Take the Picture

Firmly holding the camera, turn the focusing ring until your subject is clearest and gently press the shutter button all the way down.

There is always the chance of camera movement at speeds below 1/60 sec. with hand-held photography.

Sharply Focused   *Subject Blurred*

8 Rewind the Film

Once all the pictures have been taken, press in the rewind button. (You can tell you're at the end because the film advance lever will not turn all the way, if at all. Do not force it!)

Unfold the rewind crank and turn in the direction of the arrow until the frame counter shows "S".

Open the back cover and remove the film cartridge.

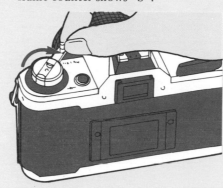

✳ Pre-shooting checklist

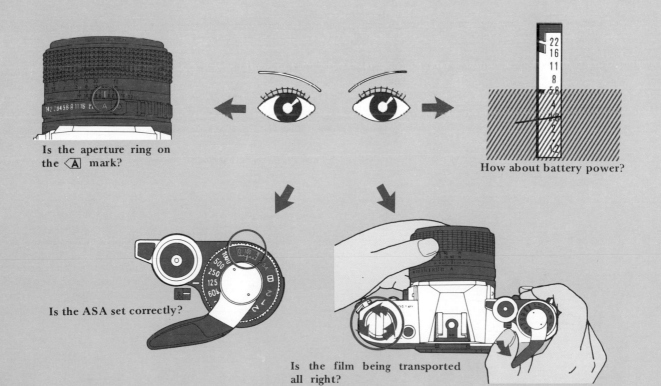

Is the aperture ring on the ⟨A⟩ mark?

How about battery power?

Is the ASA set correctly?

Is the film being transported all right?

After loading its four penlight batteries, slide the unit all the way into the accessory shoe from the back and tighten the screw at the base.

Leave the lens' aperture ring on the Ⓐ mark.

Except for B, the shutter-speed dial can be set anywhere.

When using a Canon A series Speedlite on the AE-1, both the aperture and shutter speed will be automatically set for correct exposure as soon as the pilot lamp comes on.

On the back of the Speedlite, set the ASA to match that set on the camera.

Choose either the red or green automatic aperture depending on the photographic conditions (such as depth of field and camera-to-subject distance.)

Press the shutter button half-way and if the aperture value you have selected (2.8 or 5.6 at ASA 100) is indicated in the viewfinder, go ahead and take the picture.

Aperture Selection Switch

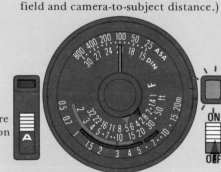

Main Switch

When the pilot lamp lights up after the unit has been turned on, everything is all right.

1 Set the Aperture Ring and Selector Dial

While pressing the aperture ring lock button, turn the ring off the "A" mark.

Turn the selector dial to Ⓐ.

First, mount the lens on the body as shown on page 52.

Once the aperture ring is off the "A" mark, it cannot be turned back there unless the lock button is pushed.

To take off Ⓐ, the lock button in the center of the dial must be pushed while turning the dial.

2 Load the Battery

Open the battery chamber cover.

Insert the battery, lower end first, and press on the upper end to snap in place. Look at the diagram inside the battery chamber to make sure you don't get the poles mixed up.

3 Check the Battery

Press the battery check button while looking in the viewfinder.

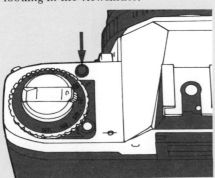

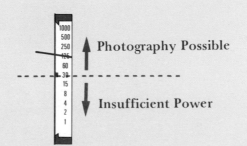

Photography Possible

Insufficient Power

The camera will not operate if battery power is too low.

4 Set the ASA

Turn the ASA dial while pushing in the lock button. The dial will be locked as soon as you let go of the button.

5 Load the Film

Lift up the rewind crank to open the back cover and drop in the film cartridge, making sure that the glossy side is up.

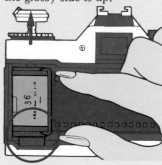

Pull the film across the camera and insert the end in one of the slots on the take-up spool.

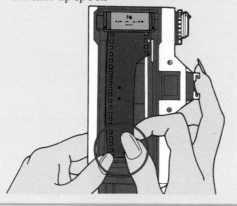

Advance the film one frame by slowly throwing the film advance lever. Make sure the film perforations and sprockets have engaged at the parts that are circled.

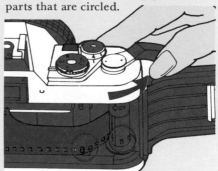

If there is no slack in the film, shut the back cover.

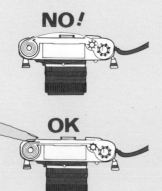

By pushing the shutter button and throwing the advance lever repeatedly, advance the film to the first frame.

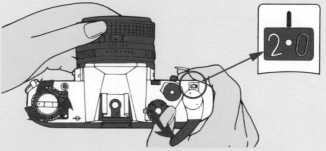

If the film rewind knob turns when you throw the film advance lever, all is O K.

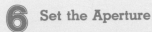 **Set the Aperture**

Choose the proper aperture by using the below chart as a reference.

Turn the aperture ring and set it on the value you have decided upon.

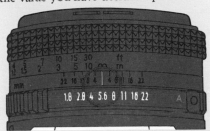

Check the exposure by looking in the viewfinder and pushing the shutter button half-way.

Overexposure warning mark (stop-down more)

Hand-held photography possible

Photography possible though camera movement may occur. Use of tripod or Speedlite recommended.

Underexposure warning mark (use a larger aperture or B (BULB)).

Take the Picture

Turn the focusing ring until the subject is clearest, hold the camera firmly and gently press the shutter button.

There is always the chance of camera movement at speeds below 1/60 sec. with hand-held photography.

Out of Focus   *In Focus*

8 Rewind the Film

When every picture in the roll has been taken, push in the rewind button.

Unfold the rewind crank and rotate in the direction of the arrow.

Once all the film has been rewound, lift up on the crank to open the back cover and remove the film cartridge.

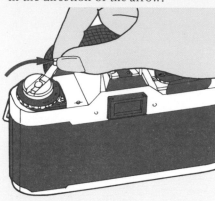

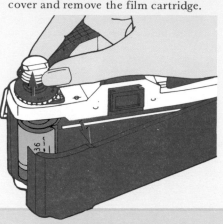

✳ Pre-shooting Checklist

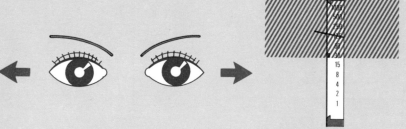

Is the aperture ring off the ⟨A⟩ mark?

Is there enough battery power?

Is the selector dial set on ⟨A⟩ ?

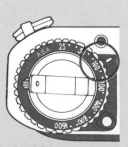

Is the ASA set correctly?

Is the film being advanced correctly?

Set the ASA to that set on the camera.

Choose either the red or green apertures according to the photographic conditions (such as depth of field and camera-to-subject distance.)

Turn the aperture ring on the lens to the aperture value chosen on the flash.

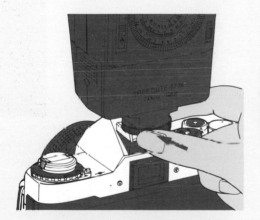

Leave the selector dial on Ⓐ.
Turn the unit on and when the pilot lamp lights up, you are all set to take the picture.

Press the shutter button half-way and if 60 (the synchronized shutter speed for flash is 1/60 sec.) is indicated in the viewfinder, everything is O K.

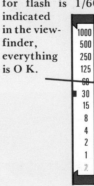

7.5mm Fisheye

15mm Fisheye

20mm

50mm

24mm

28mm

35mm

Sharpness, beautiful color, various effects, a perfect match for the A series cameras. That's what you get with Canon's lenses. As you can see from the photos on this page, each kind of lens has its own special feeling. Choose the ones that give you the most satisfaction. The number of experiences you encounter is directly proportionate to the variety of lenses that makes up your system.

300mm

200mm

20

100mm

400mm

600mm

21

1200mm

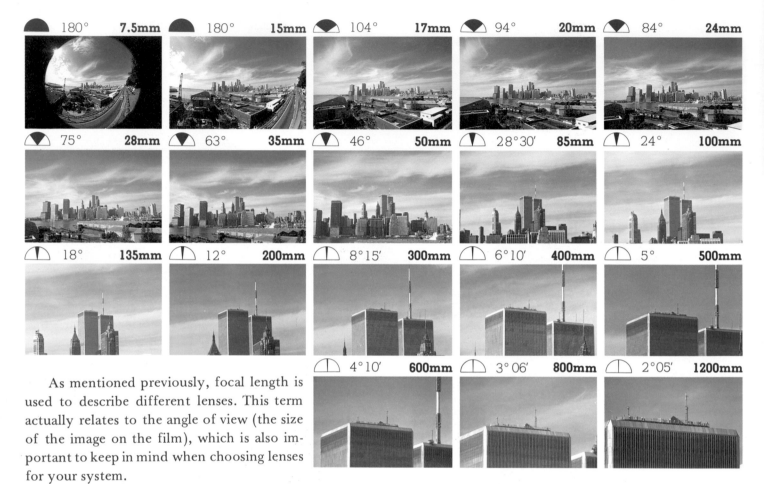

180° **7.5mm**	180° **15mm**	104° **17mm**	94° **20mm**	84° **24mm**
75° **28mm**	63° **35mm**	46° **50mm**	28°30' **85mm**	24° **100mm**
18° **135mm**	12° **200mm**	8°15' **300mm**	6°10' **400mm**	5° **500mm**
		4°10' **600mm**	3°06' **800mm**	2°05' **1200mm**

As mentioned previously, focal length is used to describe different lenses. This term actually relates to the angle of view (the size of the image on the film), which is also important to keep in mind when choosing lenses for your system.

You should first think about your shooting position and what you want to include in a picture. Will you be close to a subject but want to get as much as possible into the picture or will you be far away yet want to make your subject the main part of the picture? For any contingency, a wide assortment of lenses is best. Since a wide-angle gets a lot of things into the picture even at close distances, one of those is recommended. On the other end of the scale, a telephoto is necessary

New Fisheye 7.5mm f/5.6

FL 1200mm f/11

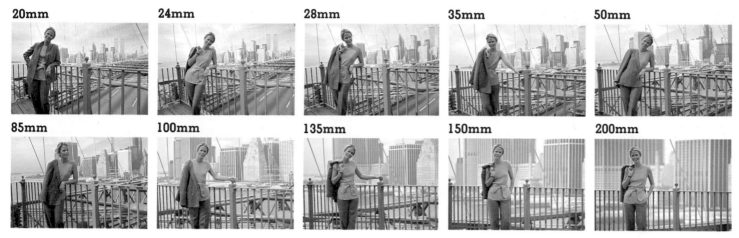

Focal Distance and Angle of View.

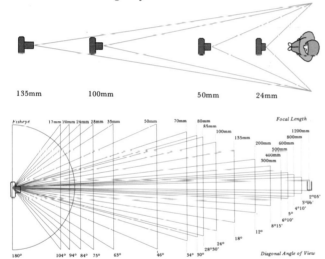

view between lenses when the photographer stands in the same spot and uses the same aperture.

There is another natural effect of using different lenses that must be taken into account. Perspective refers to the feeling, or lack thereof, of distance between the subject and other objects in the photo. For instance, try photographing a subject using different lenses so that it stays the same size. The longer the focal length of the lens, the farther away from the subject you have to go. But what happens to the background? It changes completely. With telephoto lenses, it actually looks like the background and subject are one; there is little feeling of distance even though they may be miles apart. And the background does not look in focus, thus accentuating the subject. The same sort of phenomenon holds true for the foreground as well.

if you are standing far away and want to make a particular subject stand out. To give you a better idea, the pictures on this page show the differences in angle of

New FD 20mm f/2.8

New FD 200mm f/4

Canon New FD Lens System Performance Chart

On the right is a chart of all Canon's lenses currently on the market. It shows everything from lens composition to the names of available accessories. Of course, you don't have to buy all 50 lenses to get yourself a good system. One representative lens from each group would suffice; in fact, not even that many are necessary. You should choose the lens or lenses that most fit your budget and the kind of pictures you take. The problem of what lenses are best for what occasion is explained in detail on the following pages, along with an in-depth description of each lens group. The best way to pick a lens, though, is to go to your local dealer and mount one on your camera. There's nothing like the real thing!

- Step Up Ring 52-55 is available to change filter diameter from 52mm to 55mm.
- The Extender FD2X-A is for lenses of 300mm or above. It is a rear converter that doubles focal length.
- Extender FD2X-B is for lenses up to 300mm. It is a rear converter that doubles focal length.
- L lenses are professional types that incorporate special optical glass, aspherical surfaces and other improvements.
- ∗ Indicates that this product will be available in the near future.

Name	Type	Construction
New Fisheye 7.5mm f/5.6	Circular Fisheye	8-11
New Fisheye FD 15mm f/2.8	Full-frame Fisheye	9-10
New FD 17mm f/4	Super Wide-angle	9-11
New FD 20mm f/2.8	Super Wide-angle	9-10
New FD 24mm f/1.4L	Wide-angle (Aspherical)	8-10
New FD 24mm f/2	Wide-angle	9-11
New FD 24mm f/2.8	Wide-angle	9-10
New FD 28mm f/2	Wide-angle	9-10
New FD 28mm f/2.8	Wide-angle	7-7
New FD 35mm f/2	Wide-angle	8-10
New FD 35mm f/2.8	Wide-angle	5-6
New FD 50mm f/1.2L	Standard (Aspherical)	6-8
New FD 50mm f/1.2	Standard	6-7
New FD 50mm f/1.4	Standard	6-7
New FD 50mm f/1.8	Standard	4-6
FD 55mm f/1.2 Aspherical	Standard (Aspherical)	6-8
FD 55mm f/1.2	Standard	5-7
New FD 85mm f/1.2L	Short Telephoto (Aspherical)	6-8
New FD 85mm f/1.8	Short Telephoto	4-6
New FD 100mm f/2	Short Telephoto	4-6
New FD 100mm f/2.8	Short Telephoto	5-5
New FD 135mm f/2	Short Telephoto	5-6
New FD 135mm f/2.8	Short Telephoto	5-6
New FD 135mm f/3.5	Short Telephoto	4-4
New FD 200mm f/2.8	Telephoto	5-5
New FD 200mm f/4	Telephoto	6-7
New FD 300mm f/2.8L	Telephoto (Fluorite and UD)	7-9
FD 300mm f/2.8 Fluorite	Telephoto (Fluorite)	5-6
New FD 300mm f/4L	Telephoto (UD)	7-7
New FD 300mm f/4	Telephoto	6-6
New FD 300mm f/5.6	Telephoto	5-6
New FD 400mm f/2.8L	Super Telephoto (UD)	8-10
New FD 400mm f/4.5 ∗	Super Telephoto	5-6
New FD 500mm f/4.5L ∗	Super Telephoto (Fluorite and UD)	6-7
New Reflex 500mm f/8	Mirror Super Telephoto	3-6
New FD 600mm f/4.5	Super Telephoto	5-6
New FD 800mm f/5.6L	Super Telephoto (UD)	6-7
FD 800mm f/5.6	Super Telephoto	5-6
FL 1200mm f/11	Super Telephoto	4-5
Focusing Unit (for FL 1200mm f/11)	—	1-2
Extender FD2X-A	—	4-6
Extender FD2X-B	—	5-7
Extender FD1.4X	—	3-4
New FD 24—35mm f/3.5L	Short Zoom (Aspherical)	9-12
New FD 28—50mm f/3.5	Short Zoom	9-10
New FD 35—70mm f/2.8—3.5	Short Zoom	10-10
New FD 35—70mm f/4	Short Zoom	8-8
New FD 35—105mm f/3.5	Short Zoom	13-15
New FD 50—135mm f/3.5	Long Zoom	12-16
New FD 70—150mm f/4.5	Long Zoom	9-12
New FD 70—210mm f/4	Long Zoom	9-12
New FD 80—200mm f/4	Long Zoom	11-15
New FD 85—300mm f/4.5	Long Zoom	11-15
New FD 100—200mm f/5.6	Long Zoom	5-8
New FD 100—300mm f/5.6	Long Zoom	9-14
New Macro FD 50mm f/3.5	Standard Macro	4-6
New Macro FD 100mm f/4	Short Telephoto Macro	3-5
New Macro FD 200mm f/4 ∗	Telephoto Macro	6-9
Macrophoto Lens 20mm f/3.5	Macrophoto	3-4
Macrophoto Lens 35mm f/2.8	Macrophoto	4-6
TS 35mm f/2.8	Tilt/Shift	8-9

| Angle of View | | | Minimum Aperture | Diaphragm Type | Distance Scale | | Photographic Magnification | Filter Diameter (mm) | Length × Max Diameter (mm) | Weight (g) | Hood Name | Hard Case Name | Soft Case Name |
Diagonal	Vertical	Horizontal			(meter)	(feet)							
180° (23mmφ)			22	Manual	—	—	—	Built-in	62 × 72	365	—	C10	B11
180°	—	—	22-A	Automatic	0.2~3·∞	0.7~10·∞	0.14	Built-in	60.5 × 76	460	Built-in	C10	B11
104°	70°30'	93°	22-A	Automatic	0.25~3·∞	0.9~10·∞	0.10	72	56 × 76.5	360	BW-72	C10	B11
94°	62°	84°	22-A	Automatic	0.25~3·∞	0.9~10·∞	0.13	72	58 × 76.5	305	BW-72	C10	B11
84°	53°	74°	16-A	Automatic	0.3~3·∞	1~10·∞	0.12	72	68 × 76.5	430	BW-72	C13	B11
84°	53°	74°	22-A	Automatic	0.3~3·∞	1~10·∞	0.11	52	50.6 × 63	285	BW-52C	B9	A9
84°	53°	74°	22-A	Automatic	0.3~3·∞	1~10·∞	0.11	52	43 × 63	240	BW-52C	B9	A9
75°	46°	65°	22-A	Automatic	0.3~3·∞	1~10·∞	0.13	52	47.2 × 63	265	BW-52B	B9	A9
75°	46°	65°	22-A	Automatic	0.3~3·∞	1~10·∞	0.13	52	40 × 63	170	BW-52B	B9	A9
63°	38°	54°	22-A	Automatic	0.3~3·∞	1~10·∞	0.17	52	46 × 63	245	BW-52A	B9	A9
63°	38°	54°	22-A	Automatic	0.35~3·∞	1.25~10·∞	0.13	52	40 × 63	165	BW-52A	B8	A9
46°	27°	40°	16-A	Automatic	0.5~10·∞	1.75~30·∞	0.13	52	50.5 × 65.5	380	BS-52	B9	A9
46°	27°	40°	16-A	Automatic	0.5~10·∞	1.75~30·∞	0.13	52	45.6 × 65.3	315	BS-52	B9	A9
46°	27°	40°	22-A	Automatic	0.45~10·∞	1.5~30·∞	0.15	52	41 × 63	235	BS-52	B8	A9
46°	27°	40°	22-A	Automatic	0.6~10·∞	2~30·∞	0.10	52	35 × 63	170	BS-52	B8	A9
43°	25°	36°	16-A	Automatic	0.6~10·∞	2~30·∞	0.11	58	55 × 75.8	575	BS-58	C10	B11
43°	25°	36°	16-A	Automatic	0.6~10·∞	2~30·∞	0.11	58	52.5 × 75.8	510	BS-58	C10	B11
28°30'	16°	24°	16-A	Automatic	0.9~10·∞	3~30·∞	0.12	72	71 × 80.8	680	BT-72	C13	B11
28°30'	16°	24°	22-A	Automatic	0.85~10·∞	3~30·∞	0.08	52	53.5 × 63	345	BT-52	C10	B11
24°	14°	20°	32-A	Automatic	1~10·∞	3.5~30·∞	0.12	52	70 × 63	445	BT-52	B12	B11
24°	14°	20°	32-A	Automatic	1~10·∞	3.5~30·∞	0.12	52	53.4 × 63	270	BT-52	C10	B11
18°	10°	15°	32-A	Automatic	1.3~20·∞	4.5~70·∞	0.13	72	90.4 × 78	670	Built-in	C13	B13
18°	10°	15°	32-A	Automatic	1.3~20·∞	4.5~70·∞	0.13	52	78 × 63	395	Built-in	B12	B11
18°	10°	15°	32-A	Automatic	1.3~20·∞	4.5~70·∞	0.13	52	85 × 63	325	Built-in	B12	B13
12°	7°	10°	32-A	Automatic	1.8~20·∞	6~100·∞	0.15	72	140.5 × 78	700	Built-in	C19	B21
12°	7°	10°	32-A	Automatic	1.5~20·∞	5~70·∞	0.15	52	121.5 × 63	440	Built-in	A17	A18
8°15'	4°35'	6°50'	32-A	Automatic	3~50·∞	10~200·∞	0.11	48	245 × 127	2,310	Built-in	Exclusive	—
8°15'	4°35'	6°50'	22-A	Automatic	3.5~50·∞	12~200·∞	0.11	34	230 × 112	1,900	Built-in	Exclusive	—
8°15'	4°35'	6°50'	32-A	Automatic	3~50·∞	10~200·∞	0.11	34	207 × 85	1,100	Built-in	Exclusive	—
8°15'	4°35'	6°50'	32-A	Automatic	3~50·∞	10~200·∞	0.11	34	204 × 85	945	Built-in	D24	—
8°15'	4°35'	6°50'	32-A	Automatic	3~50·∞	10~200·∞	0.11	58	198.5 × 65	635	Built-in	B24	A24
6°10'	3°30'	5°10'	32-A	Automatic	4~50·∞	15~200·∞	0.11	48	348 × 166	5,350	Built-in	Exclusive	—
6°10'	3°30'	5°10'	32-A	Automatic	4~50·∞	13~200·∞	0.11	34	287.5 × 102	1,415	Built-in	Exclusive	—
5°	2°45'	4°	32-A	Automatic	5~50·∞	20~200·∞	0.14	48	395 × 128	2,610	Built-in	Exclusive	—
5°	2°45'	4°	8	Fixed	4~50·∞	15~200·∞	0.14	34	146 × 90	705	Built-in	Exclusive	—
4°10'	2°20'	3°30'	32-A	Automatic	8~100·∞	27~300·∞	0.08	48	462 × 154	3,750	Built-in	Exclusive	—
3°06'	1°40'	2°35'	32-A	Automatic	14~100·∞	45~300·∞	0.06	48	557 × 154	4,230	Built-in	Exclusive	—
3°06'	1°40'	2°35'	22-A	Automatic	14~100·∞	45~300·∞	0.06	48	567 × 149	4,300	Built-in	Exclusive	—
2°05'	1°10'	1°40'	64	Manual	40~300·∞	130~100·∞	0.04	—	567.5 × 128	3,100	Built-in	Exclusive	—
—	—	—	—	—	—	—	—	48	285.5 × 108	3,100	—	—	—
—	—	—	—	—	—	—	—	—	35.2 × 64	210	—	Exclusive	—
—	—	—	—	—	—	—	—	—	43.9 × 64	240	—	—	—
—	—	—	—	—	—	—	—	—	34.6 × 64	210	—	Exclusive	—
84°~63°	53°~38°	74°~54°	22-A	Automatic	0.4~3·∞	1.5~10·∞	0.08~0.11	72	86.6 × 76.5	495	BW-72	C13	B13
75°~46°	46°~27°	65°~40°	22-A	Automatic	1~10·∞	3.5~30·∞	0.03~0.05	58	99.5 × 69	470	W-69B	B15	B13
63°~34°	38°~19°30'	54°~29°	22-A	Automatic	1~10·∞	3.5~30·∞	0.04~0.07	58	120 × 69	545	W-69	B15	A18
63°~34°	38°~19°30'	54°~29°	22-A	Automatic	0.5~10·∞	2~30·∞	0.08~0.15	52	84.5 × 63	315	W-62	B12	B11
3°~23°20'	54°~19°20'	38°~13°	22-A	Automatic	1.5~20·∞	5~70·∞	0.028~0.08	72	108.4 × 76.5	640	BW-72B	C16	B16
46°~18°	40°~15°	27°~10°	32-A	Automatic	1.5~20·∞	5~70·∞	0.042~0.106	58	125.4 × 71.4	720	BS-58	C16	B16
4°~16°20'	19°30'~9°10'	29°~13°40'	32-A	Automatic	1.5~20·∞	5~70·∞	0.06~0.13	52	132 × 63	530	Built-in	A17	A18
4°~11°45'	19°30'~6°30'	29°~9°48'	32-A	Automatic	1.2~15·∞	4~30·∞	0.08~0.23	58	151 × 72.2	705	BT-58	C19	B21
30°~12°	17°~7°	25°~10°	32-A	Automatic	1~20·∞	3.5~50·∞	0.12~0.29	58	161 × 67.9	765	Built-in	B24	B21
30'~8°15'	16°~4°35'	24°~6°50'	32-A	Automatic	2.5~30·∞	8~100·∞	0.04~0.15	Series IX	246.8 × 94	1,830	Built-in	Exclusive	—
24°~12°	14°~7°	20°~10°	32-A	Automatic	2.5~30·∞	8~100·∞	0.05~0.10	52	167 × 63	610	Built-in	B24	B21
24°~8°15'	14°~4°35'	24°~6°50'	32-A	Automatic	2~30·∞	7~100·∞	0.06~0.18	58	207 × 72.2	835	BT-58	C24	B24
46°	27°	40°	32-A	Automatic	0.232~3·∞	0.3~10·∞	0.5	52	57 × 63	235	BW-52A	C10	B11
24°	14°	20°	32-A	Automatic	0.45~7·∞	1.48~15·∞	0.5	52	95 × 70.3	455	BT-52	B15	B13
12°	7°	10°	32-A	Automatic	0.58~10·∞	1.9~30·∞	1.0	58	182.4 × 68.8	790	Built-in	D24	—
—	—	—	22	Manual	—	—	—	22.5	20 × 32	35	—	Exclusive	—
—	—	—	22	Manual	—	—	—	22.5	22.5 × 40	60	—	Exclusive	—
3° shift 79°	38°	54°	22	Manual	0.3~3·∞	1~10·∞	0.19	58	74.5 × 67	550	BW-58	Exclusive	—

When choosing the several interchangeable lenses for your system, one important thing to keep in mind is your own personality. In other words, what kind of pictures are you most likely to take? Sports? Portraits? Scenery? For each kind of photography, there are some lenses that are generally better than others. This doesn't take into account any special effects you may want to obtain, however (like distorting a person's body by use of certain lenses.) On the right are some examples of different types of photography, and the lenses that are most suitable for them.

Scenery and Confined Spaces

Faced with a panoramic scene and want to get as much in the picture as possible? Want to exaggerate perspective? Or, are you trying to photograph a person or thing in a confined space such as a room? At times like these, you need a lens in the super-wide-angle category, a 17mm or 20mm. Their large angle of view also exaggerates features, especially of subjects at the edges of the picture and of those at very close distances.

Rows of Objects, Interiors of Vehicles, etc.

Wide-angle lenses, those having focal lengths of from 24mm to 35mm, can be used in a variety of circumstances. For instance, use one inside some mode of transportation (there are photographers who concentrate solely on taking pictures in subways). The interior will appear roomier than is actually the case, and the passengers will also be captured on film. Wide-angle lenses also give a deeper depth of field, quite advantageous if there are objects lined up in a row that you wish to photograph from one end. This is very effective for rows of buildings too: houses, skyscrapers in a big city, etc.

General Photography

For photography of almost anything that doesn't need a special technique and is not hampered by lack of space, too much distance, and so on, 50mm standard lenses will do the job. Very compact and fast (having a large maximum aperture), they can be used for practically any type of shot—portraits, landscapes, candids. Which is why most beginning photographers choose one as their first lens.

Portraits

A medium telephoto lens, one from 85mm to 135mm, is most often recommended for this type of photography. Along with giving the most natural perspective, their shallow depth of field has the effect of blurring the background, thereby making the subject stand out. They are also usually fairly fast, allowing you to work easily indoors. And since you can stand away to get the shot, such lenses help put the subject at ease.

Sports and other Action Shots

It's rare in sports when you can get right up to the action. Many times, you will be forced to stand rather far away. That's why a telephoto lens in the 200mm or 300mm range is handy. It lets you get the subject in full frame yet you don't have to get very near the action.

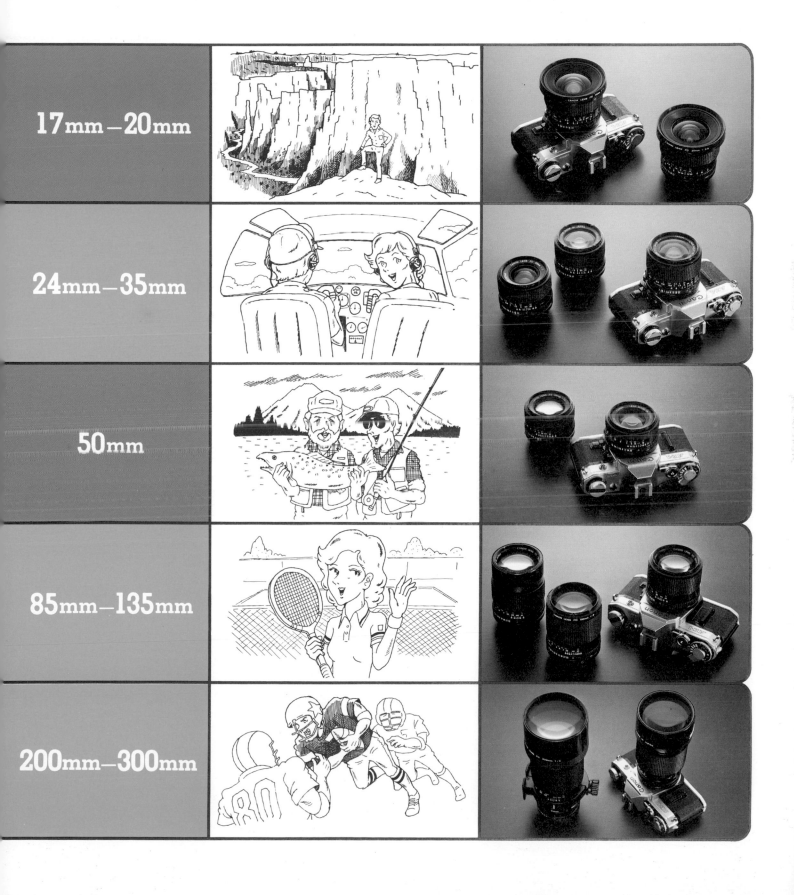

17mm–20mm

24mm–35mm

50mm

85mm–135mm

200mm–300mm

To get better color, ASA 64 film was pushed to 100. Taken with the New Fisheye FD 15mm f/2.8 at 1/125 sec., f/11.

The New Fisheye 15mm makes this boy's hand appear twice its actual size. 1/125 sec., AE.

22

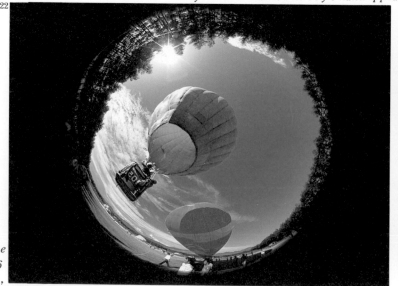

*New Fisheye
7.5mm f/5.6
at 1/125 sec.,*

New Fisheye 7.5mm f/5.6
New Fisheye FD 15mm f/2.8
New FD 17mm f/4
New FD 20mm f/2.8

Ever wonder what the world looks like through a fish's eyes? Actually, fish can see in a complete circle, or 180°. An SLR owner can get the same effect by using a lens appropriately named, "Fisheye".

Canon has two of these lenses, the New 7.5mm f/5.6 and New FD 15mm f/2.8. The former is known as a "circular" fisheye because the image taken with it does not entirely fill up a 35mm frame. The result is a picture that, rather than rectangular, is circular. When you get your pictures back from the developer's, the frame will be as always —rectangular— but the picture itself will be circular with anything outside the circle unexposed. This docs not happen with the 15mm, though, as that lens is a "full-frame" fisheye. Since it has a 180° angle of view, just like the 7.5mm, the same bending at the edges effect is possible, although it won't be as prominent in full-frame. And for close-up shots, focusing is necessary with the 15mm, unlike for the 7.5mm which has no focusing ring. The reason why focusing is not needed for most shots taken with a fisheye lens is that the depth of field extends from near the lens to infinity. Also, since normal filters cannot be screwed onto fisheyes, both these lenses come with built-in filters, six with the 7.5mm, four with the 15mm.

If you don't desire the fisheye perspective but still want to get a lot into a picture, you can go the next step to a Canon super-wide-angle. There are also two of these, the New FD 17mm f/4 and New FD 20mm f/2.8. Just like any wide-angle, if you get right up to a subject, exaggeration of features will occur, more pronounced with these lenses than with other wide-angles. If you like shooting in cramped quarters or love panoramic scenic pictures, these two lenses are probably best.

One thing to keep in mind about fisheye and super-wide-angle lenses is this: They are special lenses and not really for everyday use. Their price is therefore above other more regular lenses. Unless you particularly like their effect, perhaps you should start out instead with a lens from the next category.

The 28mm f/2.8 came in handy in this narrow alley. 1/60 sec., AE.

23

Taken with the AE-1 and 28mm f/2.8, at 1/250 sec., AE.

Here's where a combination of the 28mm f/2.8 and Speedlite 155A proved very successful. An aperture of f/11 was used.

24

New FD 24mm f/1.4L
New FD 24mm f/2
New FD 24mm f/2.8
New FD 28mm f/2
New FD 28mm f/2.8
New FD 35mm f/2
New FD 35mm f/2.8
Extender FD 2X-B

A wide-angle lens, one of a focal length from 24mm to 35mm, can be used in a wide variety of situations, everything from the Grand Canyon to your family bathroom. The picture on the far left is a good example of how you can get right up close to a subject and yet still have the background in focus enough to be able to tell where the setting is. The bathroom scene next to the squirrel picture is also a situation where a wide-angle lens comes in handy. It would have been hard to get this kind of shot with a standard or telephoto lens.

It's because of such versatility that a wide-angle lens is practically a must for any system. Canon has a total of seven: New FD 24mm f/1.4L, New FD 24mm f/2, New FD 24mm f/2.8, New FD 28mm f/2, New FD 28mm f/2.8, New FD 35mm f/2 and New FD 35mm f/2.8. With such a selection, which is the best? From the point of view of image reproduction, color rendi-

28mm

Features

New FD 28mm f/2.8

* This most popular of wide-angle lenses with a total length of only 1-3/4 in. is even more compact than the 28mm f/2.

* Even though compact, its high resolution and high contrast are unbeatable. Its seven-group-seven-element construction, the minimum necessary, and perfect lens shape prevent all types of aberration from occurring.

* The flare problem common with wide-angle lenses is eliminated by placement of a positive lens in front and back of the aperture. The idea is for the back positive lens to correct flare occurring in the front lens group. Sharpness and clarity are guaranteed from f/2.8 to f/22.

* Great depth of field is perfect for close-range, pre-focused candid shots.

tion, etc., they are all the same—excellent. You will find one of the 28mm's to be a good choice, though. Their angle of view is such that, when used close to the subject, the sensational wide-angle feeling of a 24mm can be obtained. If you aren't so close, however, the more subdued effects of a 35mm (a lens many photographers use as their standard) result. Above is a description of one of these 28mm lenses.

The New FD 50mm f/1.8 at 1/125, AE.

50mm

New FD 50mm f/1.4
New FD 50mm f/1.8
FD 55mm f/1.2 Asphcrical
FD 55mm f/1.2
Extender FD2X-B

New FD 50mm f/1.8

* The most compact and lightweight lens in Canon's interchangeable lens system, you can hardly sense the difference when it's attached.

* One of the most economical and easy-to-handle lenses.

* Its maximum aperture presents no design problems so that sharp images are assured and the cost is held down to a minimum.

A standard lens quite often makes up the nucleus of a photographer's lens system. The reason for this is three-fold. First, the standard lens is usually very compact. Second, it tends to be faster than lenses of other categories, adding to its versatility. Finally, a standard lens, with an angle of view of 46° or 43° depending on the focal length, is the lens that gives an image most closely corresponding to that of the human eye. The scene through one of these lenses therefore appears very natural.

Canon gives you a choice of four standard lenses: New FD 50mm f/1.4 New FD 50mm f/1.8, FD 55mm f/1.2 ASPHERICAL and FD 55mm f/1.2. These latter two are among the fastest in the Canon lens system. The aspherical lens is a product of technology developed by Canon to give image quality that even the pickiest professional can admire. It is, of course, priced accordingly. Most photographers find that the f/1.8 lens is just right. It offers all the speed you ever really need at an entirely affordable price.

Versatile, compact, inexpensive. A standard lens is a good start into the exciting world of Canon interchangeable lenses.

Without the 135mm f/2.8 lens for this picture, you'd be standing in the water. 1/60 sec., AE.

The 135mm f/2.8 really emphasizes the sun sparkling off the water. 1/250 sec., AE.

This model stands out because the 135mm lens softly blurs the background. 1/250 sec., AE.

26

New FD 85mm f/1.2L
New FD 85mm f/1.8
New FD 100mm f/2
New FD 100mm f/2.8
New FD 135mm f/2
New FD 135mm f/2.8
New FD 135mm f/3.5
New FD 200mm f/2.8
New FD 200mm f/4
FD 300mm f/2.8 Fluorite
New FD 300mm f/4L
New FD 300mm f/4
New FD 300mm f/5.6
Extender FD2X-A
Extender FD2X-B

135mm

Features

New FD 135mm f/2.8

* A compact, lightweight telephoto, this lens measures a mere 3 in. and is the shortest of Canon's telephotos.

* With a minimum aperture of f/2.8, this lens exhibits the beauty and attraction of blurred backgrounds well.

* Even though compact, there is no loss in performance.

* Spherical aberration (leading to unsharp images) is corrected and flare (resulting in ghost images) is eliminated, ensuring high contrast.

Sometimes it's advantageous not to get too close to your subject. When taking portraits, this is especially true as the farther away you are, the more at ease the subject will be. That is just one reason why a short telephoto lens is a welcome addition to any system. Another is that such a lens gives an undistorted portrait, unlike a wide-angle or even a standard lens that tend to exaggerate features when used up close.

In this group of lenses, Canon gives you an assortment of 12 to choose from. If medium-distance portrait photography is all you're aiming for, either of the two 85mm ones would be practical choices. Or, if you like fairly long-distance nature and sports shots, there

are four 300mm lenses available. And in between are two each of focal lengths 100 and 200mm and three of 135. So which should you choose?

A compact compromise that makes a good portrait lens and also gives the telephoto effect is either the New FD 135mm f/2, New FD 135mm f/2.8 or New FD 135mm f/3.5. The f/2.8 is described above. And if you don't think a short telephoto is powerful enough, consider that you can attach the Canon Extender FD 2X-B to any lens up to 300mm (though image quality will decrease at full aperture with short focal length lenses). This gives twice the focal length (though two f/stops in exposure are lost.) Thus, a 135mm lens actually becomes a 270mm. Quite a handy way to increase your lens power.

The flaming sunset emphasized by the FL 1200mm f/11 adds excitement to an everyday cityscape. 1/1000 sec., AE.

400mm

Features

FD 400mm f/4.5

* This is the first lens in the Canon system to employ rear focusing. Its compactness and improved performance has expanded the realm of hand-held photography from 300mm to 400mm.
* Use of special low-dispersion glass for reduction of chromatic aberration gives high resolution and contrast.
* A combination of large maximum aperture (for this type of lens) and vari-pitch focusing that holds down image movement speed at far distances makes for easy focusing.
* With a minimum shooting distance of 13 ft., small, insertable filters and other features, this lens is a favorite of professionals.

FD 400mm f/4.5
FD 500mm f/4.5L
New Reflex 500mm f/8
FD 600mm f/4.5
FD 800mm f/5.6L
FL 1200mm f/11
Focusing Unit (for FL 1200mm f/11)
Extender FD 2X-A

There will undoubtedly be times when a photographic situation necessitates bridging even more distance between you and the subject than can be covered by a short telephoto. Examples could include a shot of a baseball pitcher from the bleachers, full-frame pictures of dangerous wild-life or photos like the one on the opposite page of bright orange sunsets or sunrises. Such cases require long telephoto lenses, the kind that have focal lengths of over 300mm.

The six lenses of this group offered by Canon include: FD 400mm f/4.5, FD 500mm f/4.5L, New Reflex 500mm f/8, FD 600mm f/4.5, FD 800mm f/5.6L and FL 1200mm f/11. With such power as these lenses provide, you'll be able to stand so far away from the subject, it'll never become aware of your presence. They also give the ultimate in telephoto effects: flattened perspective, blurring of foregrounds and backgrounds due to shallow depth of field and narrowness in angle of view. The trade-off for such performance, however, is this: These lenses are big. To get pictures of any decent sharpness requires setting up a tripod. So you should allot enough time to set things up before you have to shoot.

The 28—50mm zoom's variable focus length here enables perfect framing. 1/250 sec., AE.

This night scene was captured at a speed of 1/2 sec., AE with the 28—50mm zoom.

The 35—70mm f/2.8—3.5, 1/125 sec., AE.

Several lenses in one, yet surprisingly compact. Including a zoom lens into your system will help solve a dilemma that perhaps by now you realize exists: How can one carry around enough lenses to satisfy the de-

mands of every situation?

Of course there are gadget bags you can buy to carry your equipment in but unless you get a fairly bulky

New FD 24—35mm f/3.5L
New FD 28—50mm f/3.5
New FD 35—70mm f/2.8—3.5
New FD 35—70mm f/4
Extender FD2X-B

ZOOM 35 — 70mm

Features

New FD 35—70mm f/4

* Extremely economical, this standard zoom is very popular among amateurs.

* Due to a maximum aperture of f/4, this lens is the most compact in this group.

* Easy to use, compact and inexpensive, this lens is a delightful means of experiencing the different effects of a wide-angle, standard and telephoto lens.

one, not many lenses will fit. This is where a zoom lens may be of some help.

Such a lens has varying focal lengths which means that it can be two, three or even four different lenses in one. You can change its focal length at will by just turning or sliding a ring in order to get the composition you desire. And even while changing, focus will remain the same. Which is why zooms are particularly advantageous for sports photography and journalism where speed is of the essence.

Canon has two groups of zooms, short and long. It may not seem that the short ones cover much of a range until you notice that the New FD 24—35mm f/3.5L, New FD 28—50mm f/3.5, New FD 35—70mm f/2.8—3.5, and New FD 35—70mm f/4 all contain three single-focal-length lenses. As for which of Canon's four short zooms to purchase, the 35—70mm f/4 is recommended as it covers three ranges —wide-angle, standard and the beginnings of telephoto— and is inexpensive enough for the amateur to afford.

35mm

50mm

70mm

70mm

The 80—200mm f/4 zoom lens makes the Golden Gate Bridge appear lots shorter than it actually is due to a shallow depth of field. 1/250 sec., AE.

If you want the power of several telephoto lenses along with the versatility afforded by a zoom, Canon has five long zoom lenses that satisfy your demand. These lenses are: the New FD 70—150mm f/4.5, New FD 80—200mm f/4, New FD 100—200mm f/5.6, New FD 100—300mm f/5.6 and FD 85—300mm f/4.5.

As you can see, with one each of a short and long zoom in your possession, you could cover what it would take six or seven lenses to do otherwise. So you may wonder, "If zooms are so convenient, then why purchase any single-focal-length lenses?" Actually, zoom lenses have a couple of disadvantages. One is their comparatively small maximum apertures which prohibit using them in any but the most optimum of lighting conditions (of course, using a flash unit might rectify that problem, provided the shooting distance is fairly short). Another is that, especially in the short zoom

The New FD 80—200mm f/4 at 1/250 sec., AE.

New FD 70—150mm f/4.5
New FD 100—200mm f/5.6
New FD 100—300mm f/5.6
New FD 80—200mm f/4
FD 85—300mm f/4.5
Extender FD2X-A
Extender FD2X-B

range, they are quite a bit bigger than the single-focal-length lenses they replace. However, when you consider that the alternative is to carry around a whole slew of lenses, maybe this isn't such a disadvantage after all. You can also get some special effects with zooms. Panning shots are always popular (with the telephotos as well). Then there is a technique called "racking". This is done by changing the focal length during an exposure, usually a fairly long one, giving the effect of the scenery jumping out at you, as can be seen in some of the pictures in this book.

Find the zoom lenses attractive? Maybe you should think about building your lens system around a couple. Try, for instance, the New FD 35—70mm f/4 and New FD 80-200mm f/4. With the wide-angle, standard and telephoto ranges taken care of, you will have room for one or two of the special lenses introduced on page 87.

ZOOM 70—150mm

Features

New FD 70—150mm f/4.5

* Including the single-lens focal lengths of 85mm, 100 mm, and 135mm with the added bonus of the standard 70mm and telephoto 150mm not available in standard lenses, this lens has a zooming ratio of 2.14X for great versatility.

* Change in aberrations is held down to a bare minimum by special arrangement of optical elements.

* Both zooming and focusing can be performed with one ring.

* A simple lens barrel construction makes focusing adjustment easy and gives this lens its high cost-performance.

New FD 70—150mm f/4.5 on the AV-1 at f/4.5, AE.

The Leaning Tower of Pisa effect. How this kind of shot would normally look. (left)

The corrected version shot with the TS 35 mm at 1/125 sec., f/11. (right)

Record grooves, enlarged eight times by the Macrophoto Lens 20mm f/3.5 and Bellows FL, f/16. For the left side, a blue gelatin filter was used; for the right, a red one.

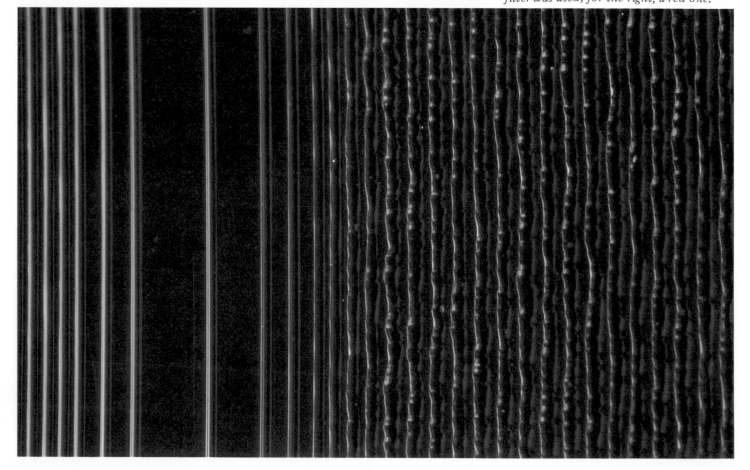

New Macro FD 50mm f/3.5   TS 35mm f/2.8
New Macro FD 100mm f/4   Extension Tube FD25-U
Macrophoto Lens 20mm f/3.5   Extension Tube FD50-U
Macrophoto Lens 35mm f/2.8

Now that you have been introduced to Canon's basic lenses, there is something you should know: all lenses, no matter who makes them, have certain limitations. The problem is minimum focusing distance. You can only get so close before the picture starts to blur. So, if you want to take a close-distance shot of some subject, you're out of luck. Unless, that is, you have a Macro lens.

This kind of lens, the New Macro FD 50mm f/3.5 and New Macro FD 100mm f/4 in Canon's case, lets you get extremely close to a small subject so that it appears on the film as if it is almost life-size. Actually, that's not far from the truth as both these lenses give 1/2 life-size magnification by themselves, life-size when used with Extension Tube FD 25-U and FD 50-U respectively (separate accessories that can also be used on other lenses). Another advantage is that they can also be used as you would normally use lenses of their focal lengths. In other words, the Macro 50mm can also be used as a standard lens, the 100mm as a telephoto.

Of course, these lenses also have limits to their minimum focusing distances. If you want even bigger magnifications, Canon Macrophoto lenses are available. These small lenses are for use with a special unit called a bellows, which is described in Part 4. The Macrophoto Lens 20mm f/3.5 gives magnifications of between 4X and 10X (four to ten times life-size) and the Macrophoto Lens 35mm f/2.8 enables 2X to 5X magnification. Although this kind of photography is a bit tricky, the rewards are mind-boggling indeed.

When you go to photograph buildings, you may encounter another problem with wide-angle or standard lenses. Since you may have to lean back to get the whole thing or even just part of it in the picture, the object becomes no longer parallel to the film plane. The building will therefore appear to be tilting in the picture. To rectify this problem, Canon makes a special TS lens (for Tilt/Shift). By special controls, this lens can shift right or left, up or down to correct the tilting phenomenon and make the building stand upright. By another knob you can also tilt the lens. This feature is used to improve depth of field when shooting at an angle to a wall, fence or other such object. Normally, even if you can increase depth of field by controlling the aperture, it will not be enough for this kind of shot. And exposure problems could result since such a small aperture must be used. The tilt mechanism increases depth of field independent of the aperture, giving you more versatility. The TS lens can also rotate on its mount so that you can tilt and shift horizontally and vertically.

In addition to the above lenses, Canon offers professional types as well that have design improvements to compensate for certain kinds of aberrations. They can be identified by the letter L after their names and a red ring around the front of the lens. When you see this mark, you know that special optical glass, aspherical surfaces and other improvements have been incorporated.

❶ New Fisheye 7.5mm f/5.6
❷ New Fisheye FD 15mm f/2.8
❸ New FD 17mm f/4
❹ New FD 20mm f/2.8
❺ New FD 24mm f/1.4 L
❻ New FD 24mm f/2
❼ New FD 24mm f/2.8
❽ New FD 28mm f/2
❾ New FD 28mm f/2.8
❿ New FD 35mm f/2
⓫ New FD 35mm f/2.8
⓬ TS 35mm f/2.8
⓭ New FD 50mm f/1.4
⓮ New FD 50mm f/1.8
⓯ New Macro FD 50mm f/3.5 w/Extension Tube FD 25-U
⓰ FD 55mm f/1.2 ASPHERICAL
⓱ FD 55mm f/1.2
⓲ New FD 85mm f/1.2 L
⓳ New FD 85mm f/1.8
⓴ New FD 100mm f/2
㉑ New FD 100mm f/2.8
㉒ New Macro FD 100mm f/4 w/Extension Tube FD 50-U
㉓ New FD 135mm f/2
㉔ New FD 135mm f/2.8
㉕ New FD 135mm f/3.5
㉖ New FD 200mm f/2.8
㉗ New FD 200mm f/4
㉘ FD 300mm f/2.8 FLUORITE

㉙ New FD 300mm f/4 L
㉚ New FD 300mm f/4
㉛ New FD 300mm f/5.6
㉜ FD 300mm f/5.6 FLUORITE
㉝ New FD 24—35mm f/3.5 L
㉞ New FD 28—50mm f/3.5
㉟ New FD 35—70mm f/2.8—3.5
㊱ New FD 35—70mm f/4
㊲ New FD 70—150mm f/4.5
㊳ New FD 80—200mm f/4
㊴ New FD 100—200mm f/5.6
㊵ New FD 100—300mm f/5.6
㊶ FD 400mm f/4.5
㊷ FD 500mm f/4.5 L
㊸ New Reflex 500mm f/8
㊹ FD 600mm f/4.5
㊺ FD 800mm f/5.6L
㊻ FL 1200mm f/11
㊼ Focusing Unit

㊽ Extender FD 2x-A
㊾ Extender FD 2x-B
㊿ Gelatin Filter Holder
51 Filters
52 Lens Hoods
53 Lens Caps
54 Dust Caps

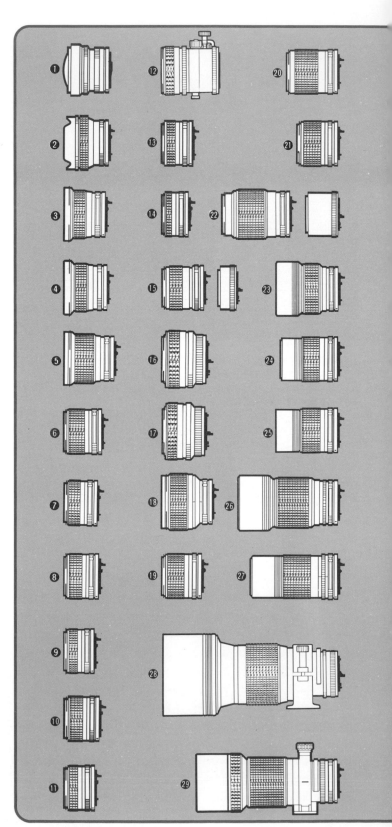

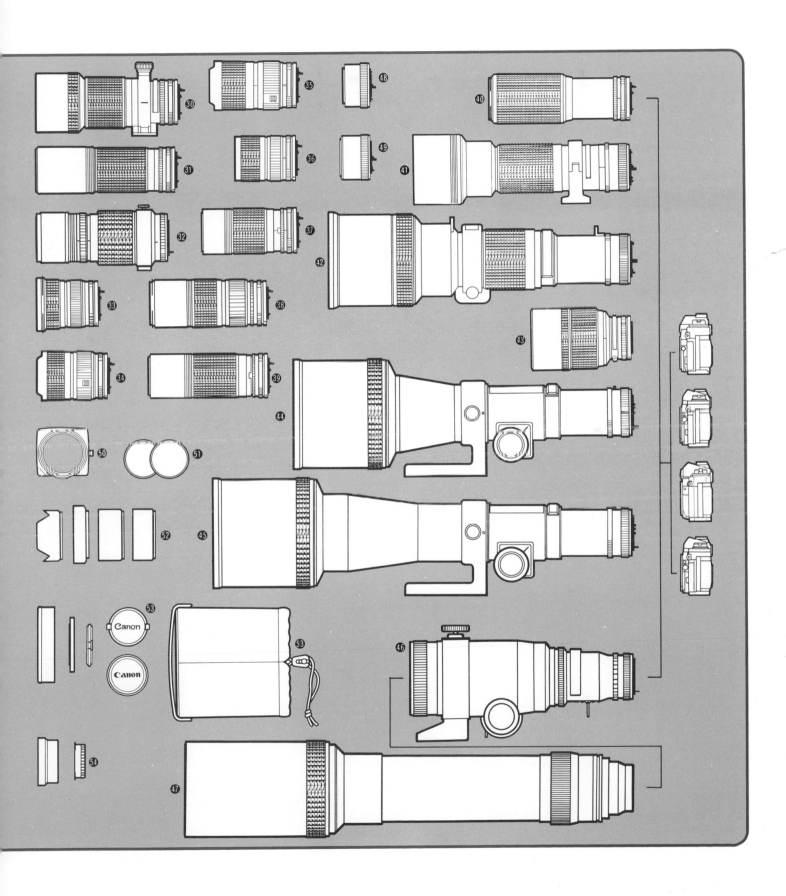

A Power Winder A action sequence taken with the New FD 17mm f/4 at 1/1000 sec., AE.   28–31

POWER WINDER A

As you have already learned, it is important for a photographer to capture the decisive moment if better-than-average pictures are desired. This moment is the climax of any type of action, and it doesn't necessarily have to be super-fast. It can take place either indoors or outdoors, too.

For the latter, a subject that immediately comes to mind is sports. For instance, a pole vaulter at the apogee of his vault is a study in beauty and grace. To capture this split second, screw the Power Winder A into the bottom of the camera and turn it on. Either release the shutter at the moment of climax or several frames before. For the latter, all you have to do is keep pressing the shutter button as the Power Winder A automatically winds the film and cocks the shutter. (Be careful not to hold in the shutter button too long lest all your film gets used up!) In this manner, you will get a group of pictures that shows the continuous flow of action, sort of like a home movie.

The same is possible indoors as well, by using the Power Winder A along with a Speedlite as long as the subject is close. Set the Speedlite in accordance with the instructions in this section. All else is automatic as both the flash unit and Power Winder A connect with the A series camera's electronics to give proper exposure.

32

The Power Winder A/Speedlite 177A combination captures the action indoors. Taken with the New FD 50mm f/1.4 at 1/60 sec. ^{33–36}

POWER WINDER A+SPEEDLITE 177A

By the way, when shooting outdoors with the Power Winder A, the camera can be set for any shutter speed but B. However, the slower the speed, the longer the time it takes for the unit to wind the film. And in order for 2 frames/sec. to be attained, a shutter speed of at least 1/60 sec. is necessary. Of course, when using the flash there's no worry on this point as the shutter speed is automatically changed to the flash synchronized speed of 1/60 sec.

Hints

1. Pick an active subject and either wait for the climax of the action or start shooting several frames before.

2. Don't hold the shutter button down more than necessary. At 2 frames per second, a lot of film can be quickly used up.

3. For comparatively slow motion where manual winding may cause you to miss a shot, use the Winder for single-frame shooting. Instead of holding the shutter button in, push and release for each picture.

4. Any shutter speed setting but B is possible, though the slower the speed, the longer the time it takes the Power Winder to wind the film. For 2 frames/sec. winding, a speed of at least 1/60 sec. is necessary.

5. Any Canon Speedlite will synchronize with the Power Winder A, though the shooting distance should be kept close. The number of flashes that are possible depends on the condition of the batteries. Giving the flash time to cool between sequences is also recommended.

6. When using in cold weather, keep the batteries warm with your body heat until they are needed.

37

1 Close-up, Photomacrography and Photomicrography

1. Close-up Lens 450, 240
2. New FD 50mm f/1.4
3. Extension Tubes FD 15-U, 25-U, 50-U
4. Extension Tube M Set
5. Macro Auto Ring
6. Bellows M
7. New Macro FD 50mm f/3.5
8. Macro Hood
9. Macrophoto Coupler FL 52
10. Lens Mount Converter B
11. Screw-type Extension Tube
12. Lens Mount Converter A
13. Macrophoto Lens 35mm f/2.8
14. Macrophoto Lens Adapter
15. Duplicator 8
16. Macrophoto Lens 20mm f/3.5
17. Duplicator 16
18. Slide Duplicator
19. Slide Duplicator Attachment
20. Bellows FL
21. Roll Film Stage
22. Duplicator 35
23. Attachment Ring
24. Auto Bellows
25. Macro Stage
26. Double Cable Release
27. Releases 30, 50
28. Camera Holder F3
29. Focusing Rail
30. Copy Stand 4 (Copy Stand 5)
31. Photomicro Unit F
32. Microphoto Hood
33. Extension Tube M5
34. F Ring 52mm
35. Handy Stand F
36. Magnifier
37. Angle Finder A2
38. Angle Finder B

2 Electronic Film Drive and Unmanned Photography

1. Canon A-1
2. Canon AE-1
3. Canon AT-1
4. Canon AV-1
5. Ni-Cd Charger MA
6. Motor Drive MA
7. Power Winder A
8. Battery Pack MA
9. Ni-Cd Pack MA
10. Battery Magazine MA
11. Extension Cord E 1000
12. Wireless Controller LC-1
13. Remote Switch 60 MF
14. Remote Switch 60
15. Remote Switch 3
16. Time Lapse Programmer, B Unit
17. Time Lapse Programmer, A Unit

3 Flash Photography

1. Speedlite 133A
2. Speedlite 155A
3. Speedlite 177A
4. Speedlite 199A
5. Macrolite ML-1

4 Date Imprinting System

1. Data Back A

5 Viewfinder System

1. Dioptric Adjustment Lenses S
2. Eyecup 4S
3. Angle Finder A2
4. Angle Finder B
5. Magnifier S

6 Cases and Bags

1. Semi-hard Case L
2. Semi-hard Case S
3. Semi-hard Case HA-2
4. Action Case A
5. Gadget Bag G-1
6. Gadget Bag 4
7. Neck Strap 7
8. Soft Lens Case
9. Hard Lens Cases

7 Underwater Photography

1. Marine Capsule A

Note: AE-1 PROGRAM and related accessories are shown on page 66.

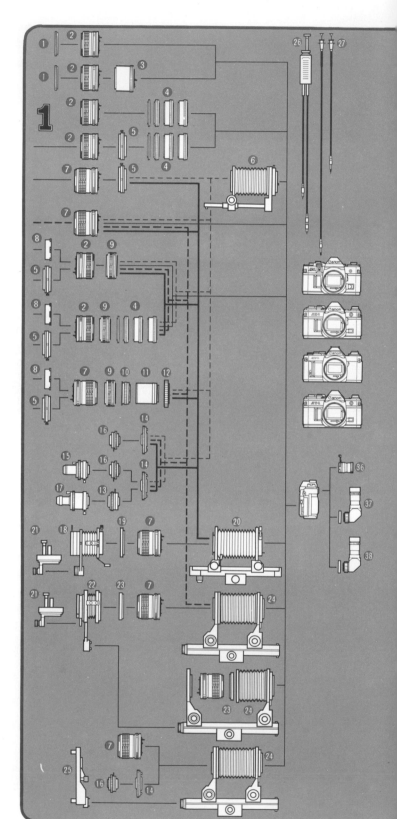

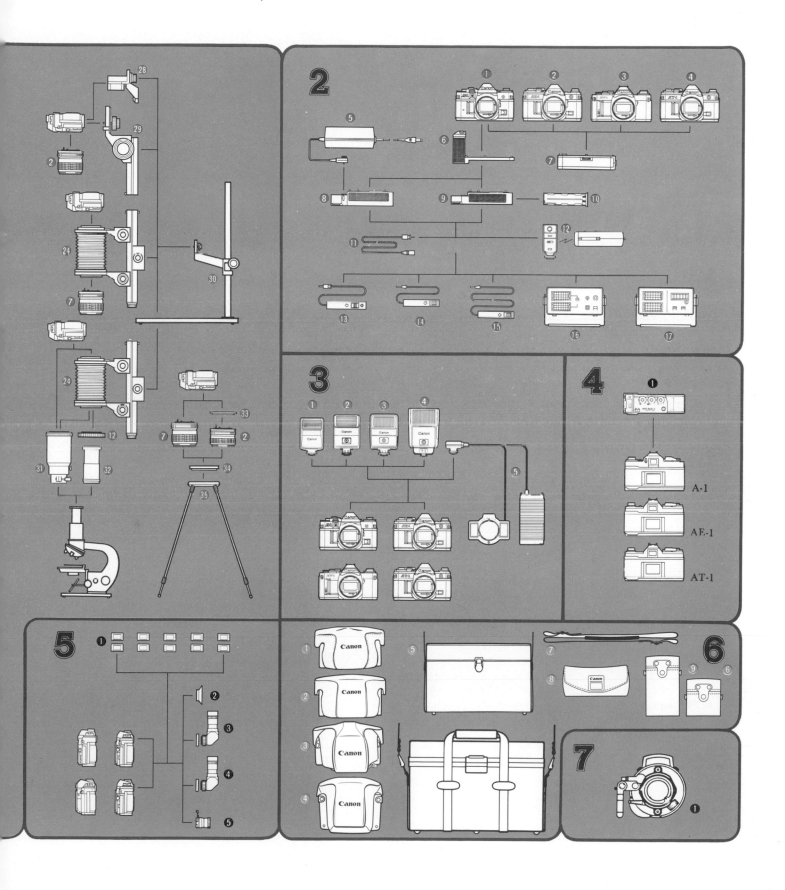

Part 4

How to hold the camera; The meaning of composition; All about lighting: natural, existing and man-made; The uses and effects of filters; Different kinds of photography and the techniques used for each; What you can do with your pictures; Specifications of the Canon A-series; Historical background of photography; Commonly asked questions and answers.

There are many techniques to taking pictures, some of which will be explained presently. One basic thing that is very important for getting good pictures should be explained here: proper holding of the camera. You may think this is something anyone can do, which it is, but some ways are better than others.

It is important when handholding a camera, first of all, to be steady. In the horizontal position, hold the camera firmly with your left hand supporting the body and lens. Press both elbows as close to your body as possible and bring the camera up to your eye so that it rests lightly against your forehead and cheek.

You shouldn't confine yourself to only horizontal pictures, though. Holding the camera vertically will often be desirable, in order to get a different angle or to fit in a tall subject. To do so, make sure at least one elbow is pressed against your body. Again, support the camera with your hand. The shutter button can either be on top or bottom. If on top, use your index finger to shoot, on bottom your thumb. Your feet should be spread slightly apart with one ahead of the other for better balance. And to be even more steady, you could lean against a wall or tree, if available. Remember: The slightest movement of hand or body during shutter release may cause blur in your photographs.

When you have thus prepared to take the picture, hold your breath and softly press the shutter button (since Canon A series cameras have electromagnetic shutter buttons, not much pressure is necessary.)

Like a composer of music or a painter, the photographer has many ways at his disposal to change the contents and feeling of his work. Of course, using the shutter speed, aperture, lenses and film are ways that we've already talked about. More simple, perhaps, is changing the arrangements or composition of the photo. You can do so in several ways: changing distance between you and the subject, shifting from one side to the opposite one, stooping or climbing to a higher vantage point, tilting the camera up or down, holding the camera vertically or horizontally.

No matter how you do it, your ultimate aim is to communicate a certain theme or idea. Things you should take into consideration for this are balance, viewpoint and framing.

Balance essentially means using the picture frame to get the best effect. Putting the main subject in the center of the picture is one way to achieve balance. As you can see from the picture below, however, it is not always true that centering your subject is the wisest course. Sometimes, more dynamic effects are created by having the subject by itself in some other part of the picture. And there is another method of creating balance as well—contrast. This is done by choosing a

You have to relax to take the picture!

subject with bright colors and surrounding it with more subdued ones, putting a detailed object against a plain or wide-open background or surrounding something dark with light, or vice versa.

Viewpoint is the position from which you look at an object. For instance, if you look down on your subject, it will appear smaller but its relationship with other objects in the picture becomes clearer. Squat down and point the camera up at something, however,

Leaning against this street lamp may allow the model to rest, but it looks as if the pole is growing right out of her head.

This is a better way to use the pole. The subject doesn't always have to be in the center.

Good composition from below.

Bad composition from above.

Too much scenery, not enough model.

Good. She fills up more of the frame.

An example of horizontal composition.

There's not enough space in front of her.

This is better. It gives the feeling she's actually looking at something.

Notice how the scene changes when the camera is held vertically.

Try photographing from various angles!

and that object becomes enormous. It also becomes isolated, thus heightening the effect of centrality of the subject. Of course, for a more natural shot, eye-level is the best.

One other thing you might consider when composing a picture is called framing. This entails using some part of your proposed picture as a frame: a hole in the wall, a window, etc. In contrast to the picture as a whole, a subject framed in this manner will stand out, but perhaps more artistically than with other methods.

There is nothing more beautiful than the effects of natural light. Catch it as it is streaming through clouds in the distance. As it makes a silhouette of a subject. As it turns a person's hair into a golden halo. Or as it dances on the water. Literally as different as night and day are the effects of light. In the early morning, it is soft and diffused, giving a red tinge to the scene. As day progresses, however, it becomes harsh and can cast bluish shadows which, if you're not careful, could ruin your picture. And then, towards evening, the sunlight becomes golden, casting long shadows, to become the blue skies of twilight. To this daily variety, add the changes of the seasons—intense light in summer, subdued in fall, stark in winter and fresh in spring—and you've got an incredible number of differing situations to think about.

An hour and a half after sunrise

The lighting at high noon

An hour and a half before sunset

You also have a choice as to where to position the light source. Although the sun, of course, cannot be physically moved, you can make it give different effects by changing your subject's relative position. For instance, if the sun is behind you, natural colors and even lighting result, though shadows will appear behind the subject who may also be squinting. On the other hand, if the light is behind that person, in other words in front of you, he/she will become blotted out as the picture is exposed for the sun. This silhouette-type effect is sometimes desirable, though it can be quite obnoxious if you're not expecting it. There is a method, explained on the next page, for taking this kind of picture so that the subject comes out with details visible.

Probably the most effective type of natural lighting is when the sun comes from the side of the subject. If you are taking a portrait, it softens the mood of the person and gives an overall feeling of three-dimensionality while making details stand out.

More than anything else, light is the means to a photographer's creative expression. Experiment with it and you'll begin to see what an all-encompassing medium photography can be.

How natural lighting can enhance a portrait. Taken with the AV-1 and 100—200mm f/5.6 zoom lens, at f/5.6.

Light reflected off the ocean often gives startling effects. The AE-1 and 70—150mm f/4.5 zoom lens, 1/250 sec.

Backlighting and the 35—70mm f/4 zoom up close give this plant a feeling of majesty. 1/250 sec. with the AE-1.

Side/backlighting adds a touch of delicacy to this otherwise ordinary flower. The AE-1 and Macro 50mm, 1/250 sec.

The lines and roundness of the face are brought out with sidelighting. AE-1 and 100mm f/2.8 lens, 1/60 sec. at full aperture.

This contrast of light and shadow makes for an interesting picture. AE-1 and 17mm f/4, 1/250 sec.

With the sun behind the subject, she becomes a mere shadow.

Corrected, the model is properly exposed.

Backlight Correction

A backlighted subject is one that has the sun, another bright light source, or a bright window to its back. In such a case, your camera will expose for the brightness of the light and not the subject, making your person, or whatever, a dark form lacking details. To correct this, the Canon AE-1 and AV-1 have a backlight control switch. Press and hold it in as you take the picture. On the AE-1, aperture will be automatically increased, on the AV-1 shutter speed will be decreased, both by 1.5 steps. This will be sufficient in most cases to render the subject visible. If, however, the sun is directly behind the subject, you may have to switch to manual operation (AV-1 excepted) and increase exposure even more. For backlight correction with the AE-1 PROGRAM, refer to page 54.

If the sun is behind your subject, or the subject is indoors in front of a window during the daytime, his or her face will definitely be underexposed unless you compensate by using the method explained on the previous page. You could also use a flash unit for this purpose. By just mounting and setting it in the normal fashion, enough light will usually be cast to offset the sunlight from the back.

Of course, this is only one use for a flash. It can also be used to correct the coloring that is the result of using daylight film under conditions for which it was not intended. We've already talked a little bit about this. If, for instance, you use daylight film indoors under tungsten lighting, all your pictures will have a red/orange cast to them. On the other hand, if the kind of lighting available is fluorescent, then a greenish/yellowish tinge will occur.

some, most amateurs prefer to do the same technique using only portable flash units. Keep the following things in mind, and good results will be yours.

Most important are the relative positions of the light source, subject and camera. Although the different combinations of these three factors are quite numerous, there are basically five patterns: Rembrandt, rim, front, top and side lighting. Examples of each are shown on the opposite page. The basic rule to remember is that with each, there is one "sun" which causes one shadow. The kind of lighting that leads to double shadows should be avoided. Rembrandt lighting refers to the emphasis of certain parts of a subject with the rest in shadow. Rim lighting is total backlighting which makes the surroundings and subject dark yet gives the latter a sunny glow. These are rather special techniques. Front, side and top are more basic. If you take a directly frontal flash picture of a person, which is the easiest as the flash unit can remain on the camera, all shadows on

Fluorescent Lighting

Daylight

Tungsten Lighting

As you know, there is special film for tungsten lighting. Changing films before the first one is finished, however, is a bothersome process. Another method for getting more natural colors is to use special correction filters. Or, you could use a flash which, regardless of the kind of lighting and film, will give fairly natural results (though if one is used with tungsten film a bluish tinge will occur). Actually, most professional photographers use a special device called a floodlamp. They use two —one to act as the main light and a weaker one for fill-in light. But since using floodlamps is quite bother-

the subject's face will be eliminated. This isn't necessarily desirable, however, as it can be too harsh and cause your subject's eyes to come out as red spots. Shots taken with the flash to one side or higher up will give natural shadows and therefore make the subject appear more three-dimensional. This technique is called modeling and can be obtained by taking the flash unit off the camera. To do this with the AE-1 and Speedlites 155A, 177A or 199A, connect the Canon Synchro Cord A to the flash. Since this is only 10 in. long, connect an extension cord (not available from Canon)

Rembrandt Lighting   **Rim Lighting**   **Front Lighting**   **Top Lighting**   **Side Lighting**

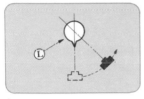

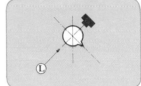

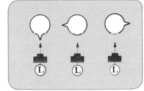

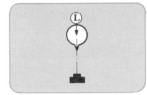

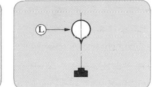

to the synchro cord and connect the whole thing to the camera's PC socket. As long as you hold the flash at approximately the same distance from the subject as when the unit was on the camera, the Speedlite's automatic functions, except for the shutter speed which you must set yourself, will be preserved. (This tech-

Further possibilities with lighting include diffused and bounced light. Both of these soften the light and give a more flattering portrait. You can do the former by putting a white tissue or Wide Adapter over the flash, the latter by tilting the head of the flash unit up towards

With a dark background, there are almost no shadows.

If the model leans against the background, shadows are unnoticeable.

Three feet away from the background and suddenly you have shadows.

Shadows appear on the right of the subject if lighting is positioned to the left

Notice how facial shadows are softened by bouncing the light off the ceiling.

nique is not possible with the AV-1 which does not have a PC socket. You have to use the Canon Hot Shoe Adapter to hook up an extension cord.) Experiment with different angles, backgrounds and contrasts and you will come up with some interesting lighting effects.

the ceiling (possible on 199A only). If you do decide to try bounce flash, make sure the ceiling is some neutral color, preferably white. Otherwise, you could end up having the color of the ceiling reflecting off the subject.

Have you ever had a half-used roll of daylight slide film in your camera and attempted to use it indoors? If so, you were probably surprised and even a bit angered to find that those indoor pictures looked yellow-orangish. As was mentioned on the previous page, a filter will correct this problem.

Actually, there are more filters than you can shake a stick at, put out by both Canon and other makers. There are basically four reasons why you might want to use filters: to improve color quality by cutting down haze, ultra-violet light, reflections, etc.; to correct color differences when a type of film is used under conditions for which it is not intended; to give special effects; to protect the lens. In the first category are three types of filters, the skylight, UV and polarizer.

The first two of these have little actual effect on your pictures. The skylight's main purpose is to weaken the bluish tone that predominates on overcast days. Absorbing ultra-violet radiation that is naturally present in the atmosphere is the purpose of the UV filter. Human beings cannot see this radiation, but it gets recorded on film as bluish haze, especially when shooting distant objects. It will not cut out haze visible to the eye, however. For that purpose, as well as to reduce or eliminate reflections and make colors richer, polarizing filters are available. These filters are rotated so that you can find the best angle for the maximum effect. With an SLR, you can tell the position at which glare, for instance, is best eliminated by just looking in the viewfinder. To give the sky a darker blue, however, you have to point the camera at the portion of the sky from whence the polarized light comes. To find this area, make a 90° angle with your index finger and thumb and point the index finger at the sun. Where your thumb points as you rotate your hand is the area of polarized light. Aiming the camera 90° to the sun's direction gives optimum results.

The effects of a polarizing filter are almost miraculous, when used properly. One problem with it, though, is called filter factor which tells you how much exposure must be increased to compensate for the amount of light reduced by a particular filter. For a polarizer, it is 2X, or one f/stop increase (remember: an increase of one step in aperture size gives double the exposure). Your Canon A series SLR, of course, automatically takes care of this change, though you should remember that a slower shutter speed than usual will be necessary in dim lighting. On the right is a chart showing the various Canon filters available and their filter factors expressed in terms of exposure differences.

There are times when high filter factors may come in handy. When you have ASA 400 film in your camera and want to take pictures at a sunny beach, for instance, or want to try long-exposure photos, normally there will be too much light for your lens and shutter speed to handle. An ND filter will then come to your rescue. Canon has six of these gray filters, ND 0.3, ND 0.6, ND4, ND4-L, ND8, ND8-L. The 0.3 allows only 50% of the normal light to strike the film whereas the 0.6 and 4 allow 25% and the 8 allows 12.5% (L-type are higher quality versions).

There is also a wide variety of other special effect filters such as Canon's Softmat filter for light diffusion, and starburst, multi-image and split-field ones made by other manufacturers. In addition, any of the colored filters from the chart can be used to render a picture totally that color,

◄ 40
Orange
15
Filter

No Filter ▲

Tungsten film with no filter ▲

Tungsten film with 85B Filter ▲

▲ *No Filter at 1/125 sec.*

▲ *ND4 Filter at 2 sec.*

41

▲ *Without a Polarizer*

▲ *With a Polarizer*

FILTER # NAME	FILM TYPE	LIGHTING	f/STOP INCREASE	SUGGESTED USES
SKY 1A	Daylight Color	Daylight	—	Used outdoors to reduce blue in shade areas, good protection for lens.
HAZE (UV-1)	Daylight Color or Black and White	Daylight	—	Reduces excess blue present in haze, marine, and mountain scenes, good protection for lens.
YELLOW 2 (#8)	Black and White	Daylight	1	Used with Black and White films for better tone separation in sky, foreground and overall contrast.
GREEN 11	Black and White	Daylight	2	Used with Black and White Pan films — ideal for outdoor portraits against sky. Renders good tone separation in foliage and natural sky appearance.
ORANGE 15	Black and White	Daylight	1-2/3	Used with all Black and White films, ideal for portraits of people with poor skin complexions when using Pan films.
RED 25A	Black and White	Daylight	3	Heavy contrast effects for architectural subjects with Pan film, used with Black and White Infra-Red film for high contrast results.
80A	Daylight Color	3200°K floods	2	Conversion of daylight color films to 3200° Kelvin tungsten lights, quartz (or professional floods).
80B	Daylight Color	3400°K floods	1-2/3	Conversion of daylight color films to 3400° Kelvin tungsten light (photo-floods).
81A	Type B Color and Daylight	Electronic flash	1/3	Used with daylight color films to balance and reduce excessive blue from electronic flash. Use outdoors to prevent excessive blue in open shade and for added warmth.
81B	Type B Color and Daylight	Electronic flash	1/3	For increased correction of the bluish cast caused by most electronic flash units.
85	Type A Color	Daylight	2/3	Used with Daylight color films, produces vibrant sunsets and adds warmth to fall-foliage scenes.
85B	Type B Color	Daylight	2/3	Converts Type B color films for outdoor daylight use. Also renders warmer effects than the #85 filter.
CCA4	Daylight Color	Daylight	1/2	Eliminates bluish tinge when shooting with daylight film under cloudy or rainy weather conditions or in the shade under fair weather conditions.
CCA8	Tungsten	Daylight	1	Used for more natural color when shooting in morning or evening light with tungsten film.
CCA12	Tungsten	Daylight	1	Used with tungsten film for shooting in sunlight (or other light source with daylight color temperature).
CCB4	Daylight	Daylight	1/2	Used with daylight film for shooting in the morning or evening light to eliminate reddish tinge.
CCB8	Daylight	Clear Flash Bulbs	1	Used with daylight film for shooting at night or indoors with clear flash bulbs.
CCB12	Daylight	Artificial Lighting	1	Used with daylight film for shooting under artificial lighting to obtain natural color tones.
FCB	Type B	All Fluorescent lighting	1	Used with Type B color films to correct yellowish-green cast caused by fluorescent lighting.
FCD	Daylight	All Fluorescent lighting	1	Used with all Daylight color films to correct the blue-green cast caused by fluorescent lighting.
ND 0.3	Color or Black and White	All sources	1	Used with all films for uniform reduction of light. Also ideal for special effects where "stop-action or a blurred background is desired". Allows 50% light transmission.
ND 0.6	Color or Black and White	All sources	2	Same as above. Allows 25% light transmission.
ND4 ND4-L	Color or Black and White	All sources	2	Same as above. Reduces light intensity to 1/4.
ND8 ND8-L	Color or Black and White	All sources	3	Same as above but twice as strong. Reduces light intensity to 1/8.
POLARIZER	All Color or Black and White	All sources	2	Used for better color saturation, greater contrast between clouds and sky and for haze penetration. Eliminates surface reflections and unwanted glare.

* The new L-type ND filters are not typical colored glass filters. Produced by evaporating a special substance on transparent glass in a high vacuum, they assure that the light intensity of each visible light ray is reduced in equal amounts for extra high-quality performance.

besides their main function of correcting for color discrepancies. Such an effect can sometimes be outstanding. And even if you have no interest in filters, buying a skylight or UV and keeping it on your lens is recommended, if for no other purpose than to protect this delicate, expensive instrument from harm.

Photography is more than just pointing your camera and shooting. Your Canon A series SLR opens up for you an incredibly rich world of photographic possibilities. The previous 100 pages of this book have given you ample examples of some of them. And you should by now have realized that there are many things to consider when starting out on a picture-taking expedition: type of film to use, appropriate lens(es), lighting, suitable accessories, etc.

Before considering these things, however, you must decide what kind or kinds of pictures you are going to end up taking. Going to a wedding? Then you'll probably need portrait lenses and perhaps special lighting or tungsten film. Going for a walk in the forest? You'd better be prepared for some dark situations; in other words, take along ASA 400 film, fast lenses and maybe even a tripod or Macrolite and Macro lens for close-up shots of insects and plants. For different types of photography, varying combinations of equipment are necessary. Moreover, there are various tricks you can use to get better-than-average results.

Most of the rest of this section is devoted to different photographic themes and the techniques needed to master them. With this knowledge and experimentation on your part, your present uncertain, haphazard photographic endeavors will take on the assured, creative air of the semi-professional.

Lighting is the key for portrait photography. A V-1 at f/5.6 with the 80—200mm zoom.

A family shot like this is great for commemorating some event. A V-1 with Speedlite 155A and 35mm f/2 lens.

The child's face is emphasized by taking the picture from above. AE-1 and 35—70mm f/2.8—3.5 zoom, 1/60 sec.

When they stand still long enough, animals make great subjects. *AE-1 and 200mm f/4 at 1/250 sec.*

The Macro 50mm enabled the photographer to get this cactus close-up without getting pricked. *0.5X magnification, f/22.*

For travel photos, a panoramic view such as this can tell the story. *AE-1 and 15mm f/2.8 fisheye, 1/250 sec.*

Delicate natural lighting turns this into something more than just a shot of some tomatoes. *AE-1 and 80—200mm f/4 zoom, 1/250.*

Long lens and fast shutter speed equal a dynamic sports shot. *AE-1 and 400mm f/4.5 lens, 1/500 sec.*

The panning technique gives a sense of action to this auto race. *AE-1 and 135mm f/2.8 lens, 1/60 sec.*

Commemorative Pictures

Since the depth of field in the foreground is about half that of the background, focusing more towards the front makes the whole group in focus.

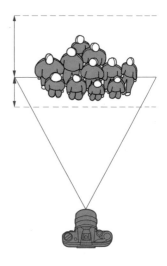

The AE-1 and 35mm f/2 lens, 1/125 sec.

The AE-1 and 24mm f/2.8 lens, 1/125 sec.

The AE-1, 35mm f/2 lens and Speedlite 155A, f/5.6.

Weddings. Family get-togethers. Birthday parties. Trips. These are just a few of the times when commemorative pictures would be highly appreciated, not only by yourself but by everyone concerned.

Your main goal should be to portray the atmosphere and feelings of the event. Many times, especially when you're on trips at the beach or in the mountains, just a picture of one of your companions will not suffice. Part of the scenery that tells where you were should also be included. At other times—parties and family get-togethers—it's the people that are important. The best thing for you to do on such occasions is to be as much a part of the festivities as possible; make you and your camera blend in rather than have the camera act as a barrier between you and the party-goers. By doing so, you will be able to get many more candid shots. Also, it is best to take pictures at different stages of the event. Before the action starts, the scene is usually quite orderly and the people's faces full of expectation, therefore more expressive. On the other hand, pictures taken during the party show how it has progressed and while both people and the scene may become rather dishevelled, they convey the atmosphere well. For weddings or other organized happenings, you should find out in advance the order of events so you can be prepared for them. Scouting out the place beforehand will enable you to be aware of any obstacle that may obstruct your view, the lighting, etc.

As for what sort of equipment to use, lenses in the focal length range of 35mm to 135mm would be good. A 35mm will enable you to get a whole group of people in one picture whereas a standard or medium telephoto will give more natural portraits of one or several people. And their relatively fast speed is useful for dim light. Very often, though, you will find that a flash will come in handy, especially for indoor or outdoor night happenings. If indoors, bounce flash will prevent "red eye" and give even illumination. There may be times when flash is not allowed, however. For such a contingency, keep plenty of high-speed film on hand.

The Data Back A

To make your commemorative pictures even more dear, Canon offers the Data Back A accessory for dating them. It replaces the back of the camera and has three dials that enable imprinting of letters, Roman numerals and Arabic numerals. All you do is set them to the desired data, and the Data Back A uses the camera's circuitry for imprintation, in the lower right-hand corner of the picture, simultaneous with exposure.   (Cannot be used on the AV-1.)

People «Portraits»

A little backlighting and the 100—200mm f/4 zoom were the ingredients of success. Taken with the AV-1 at f/4.

People are probably the most often used theme in photography. Relatives, friends or man-in-the-street, the expressions people give are worth millions of words. There are basically two types of people photography. One is portraiture and the other is candids.

The most important thing for portraiture is lighting. As mentioned previously, this factor is entirely different depending on whether you are indoors or out.

Indoors during the daytime, natural light coming through a window or door will be great illumination, especially if the day is overcast (overcast conditions make for more evenness). If you stand or sit your subject in front of a window, however, this constitutes backlighting and special exposure corrections will most likely be necessary. At night, of course, a flash is a must; the light from it or a photolamp should be reflected off the ceiling, a special reflector, an umbrella, etc. to avoid harshness. You can try shooting under regular artificial lighting as well, though it may not be bright enough to photograph without a tripod. Be careful also that the film you use matches the light source. And with ASA 400 film, though it gives you increased speed, it is grainy which may not do favor to your subject.

Outdoors, you have just the reverse problem: too much light. If the sunlight is evenly diffused, as on a cloudy day, then there is no problem. On extremely bright days such as those in mid-summer, however, the

Side lighting accentuated the features of this man's face. The AE-1 and 28mm f/2.8 lens, at 1/125 sec.

49

This Polynesian man didn't enjoy being distracted from his work to pose. The AV-1 and a 35mm f/2 lens, at f/5.6.

This French shopkeeper doesn't mind posing! The AE-1 and 50mm f/1.4 at 1/250 sec., AE.

The cow tells the story of this French farmer's life. The AV-1 and 85mm f/1.8, at f/5.6 AE.

harsh sunlight will cause the subject to squint and make shadows under the eyes and chin which will never be appreciated. To get rid of the squinting, position the subject so that the sun is to one side of the camera. To remove shadows, a flash unit is a good tool (even outdoors) as its even illumination will fill them in. And if the subject is backlighted, a flash will enable you to get proper exposure of the subject's face, yet the background will not be washed out (as would be the case if, for example, you took the picture using the backlight control switch on the AE-1).

One way to get out of using a flash for outdoor portraiture is to utilize side lighting whenever possible. As shown by some of the photographs on these two pages, such lighting gives a natural three-dimensionality to the face. And while there are shadows, they tend to complement the portrait rather than detract from it. Backlighting is also an effective technique, especially for women, as it gives their hair a golden glow, which can be quite flattering.

For portraiture, it is necessary to get people to pose. It is then your chore as the photographer to get a natural-looking picture even though the subject knows what you're up to. Communication is the key here. Establish rapport with the person and he or she will soon get used to you and your camera. Having a subject perform some action will also be beneficial.

About Reflectors

Reflectors are almost a must for portrait photographers. They are used to finely adjust studio lighting or to fill in shadows both indoors and out. You can get a reflector by either buying one or making one yourself. White poster board or a piece of cardboard covered with crumpled aluminum foil will suffice. Indeed, anything can act as a reflector, a piece of cloth, the pages of an open book, etc. Just be careful that your reflector is not colored or else that color will be transferred to your subject's face.

People «Candids»

A perfect example of zoom composition versatility. The 80—200mm f/4 zoom at 1/250 sec., AE.

Not all pictures of people have to be portraits. In fact, you will often get more interesting shots of people when they aren't looking. Pictures like this are known as candids.

The element of surprise is probably the photographer's greatest tool for this kind of photography. If the subject knows you are taking his picture, he will immediately strike an unnatural pose (unless that person happens to be a real ham). Good portrait photographers can get the subject to relax, but it sometimes takes a lot of experience to ensure success. That's why candid shots of people going about their daily business are effective. To make sure you are not noticed, zoom or telephoto lenses are necessary. Long zooms are especial-

ly helpful as they not only give you added composition freedom, but they also allow you to stand relatively far away. Take, for example, the picture of the woman drinking the milk shake. Because the photographer used the 80—200mm zoom, she was never aware of his presence and perfect framing was possible.

There will be times, of course, when you may not be able to keep your presence a secret. Though people will gradually get used to you and your camera, you can't spend time fiddling with the camera controls and expect to get good candid expressions. It is best to have these things pre-set. Decide on the shutter speed (outdoors a faster one is better to catch any momentary actions or expressions) well before you take the picture.

A Portuguese woman going about her 51
daily business. The 85mm f/1.8 at
1/250 sec., AE.

Children at play are great for candids. 52
The 100mm f/2.8 at 1/125 sec., AE.

The 24–35mm zoom at 1/250 sec., AE. 54

Although this French fisherman became 53
aware of the photographer, a good candid
shot was already in the bag. The 85mm
f/1.8 at 1/250 sec., AE.

Good subjects for candids are children. It is hard to get them to pose for portraits because their attention span in short and they don't stay still very long. If you are quick with the shutter button (the Power Winder A will help here) and on your toes, you will be able to photograph them in all their wonderful naturalness, like the picture above.

This is especially true for indoor candids where it is next to impossible to hide yourself. You will stick out like a sore thumb if you are always manipulating the controls. Pick a shutter speed (or aperture) and stay with it. Also, find a focusing range and keep within that distance. You can then concentrate on capturing the little gestures and expressions that make candid photos so realistic. And when indoors, use high-speed film because a flash unit and candid photography do not mix. You may find that even high-speed film will not enable use of faster shutter speeds. In that case, wait for lulls in the conversation to minimize subject movement.

Push-processing the Film

For indoor candids where you can't use a flash and for other dim light conditions, you can get more "speed" out of some slide films by push-processing them. Just set the ASA dial on the camera to a setting higher than the rated one. When you take the film to be developed, tell them how far the film has been pushed (underexposed). With most slides, you should limit this technique to double the rated ASA as anything over that will cause color change and increase in graininess. You should be careful with this technique to remember that the whole roll must be taken at this increased ASA. Also, many camera shops may not be able to push-process the film to your specifications. Check with them to make sure.

Landscapes

Nothing beats the Wild West for a beautiful landscape. The AV-1 and 20mm f/2.8 lens at f/11, AE.

55

A road out West, straight as an arrow, going on forever. A blazing sunset over the Pacific Ocean. A huge field full of nothing but corn stalks and a red farmhouse in the middle. Or the congestion of the Manhattan skyline. All of these are examples of landscape photography. A deft combination of natural shapes, color and light makes for outstanding photographs that everyone can admire.

Landscape photographs depend a lot on the time of day, as explained on page 100. Since the early morning light casts a golden aura over the landscape, this is a popular time. The fiery skies of sunset are also often-seen themes. You can get acceptable pictures by just pointing your AE-1, AE-1 PROGRAM or AV-1 at the

Try Different Compositions

These three pictures of the Washington Monument show well the differences in composition. In the first one, the pool of water leads the eye straight to the white monument at the end. The white color forms a sharp contrast to the gray skies. Taken from the opposite side, however, the backlighting turns the monument into a dark, almost foreboding shape. Then, closing in with a zoom shows the landscaping at its base where the subject becomes not so much the monument itself as the flags and grass around it.

56

57

Attaching a polarizer and pushing the film from ASA 64 to 125 made the blues even bluer. The AV-1 and 20mm f/2.8 lens at f/16., AE, with ASA 64 film.
AV-1 and 20mm f/2.8 at f/16, AE.

A zoom lens got this composition just right. The AE-1 and 70—150mm f/4.5 zoom,1/250 sec., AE.

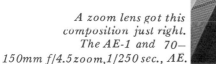

Sunsets are always favorite subjects for landscapes. The AE-1 and 28mm f/2 at 1/15 sec., AE.

scene and letting the camera do it all. For excellent landscapes, though, there are a few things to consider.

First, use of filters. A UV filter will absorb some of the ultra-violet light in the atmosphere that gives distant subjects a bluish haze. Richer colors will be obtained, which is also a result of using a polarizing filter to eliminate reflections. The kind of film you use is also a factor. Slow-speed film, for instance ASA 25 or 64, is best as it isn't as grainy as faster film, giving more sharpness. The lenses you can use cover almost the whole spectrum. While you may think that a super-wide angle would be best as it captures a lot of the scene, this is not necessarily so. Although it will include more than other lenses, it also tends to push everything into the background, thus reducing the scale of the landscape. A regular wide-angle or standard would be better as this effect is not so apparent. And a medium tele-

photo can be used to emphasize some part of the scene without losing the sense of depth of field as with longer telephotos.

Composition, more than the above things, should be your most important consideration. A simple shift in your position or camera angle could add a lot of life to a static landscape. For instance, the picture on this page of the waterfall would have been much less spectacular if the photographer had not been facing the sun. Likewise, the skyscraper picture wouldn't be any different than an ordinary picture of a building if it wasn't for the tree in the foreground.

And herein lies the key. Including some foreground object in your picture will give a sense of scale to your landscape, and thus make it appear more natural.

Travelogues

Photographs are excellent memorabilia of any trip. Many people arrange their photos of a trip and put them in an album to show friends and relatives, an effective way of relating their travel experiences. Taking slides and making a slide show (described further on pp. 142—145) is an even more effective method.

Travel photos can include almost every kind of picture: commemorative, landscape, portrait, etc. But since you will be travelling and definitely won't need lots of heavy equipment, only one SLR and a couple of lenses (or maybe one zoom) are necessary. You should probably stock up on film, however. If you intend to go out

59

What better symbol of San Francisco than the Golden Gate Bridge! The AE-1 and 50mm f/1.4, 1/250 sec., AE.

A window seat is a photographer's best friend when flying. The AE-1 and 28—50mm f/3.5 zoom, 1/125 sec., AE, with ASA 64 film pushed to 100.

Why buy a post card when you've got your camera? The AE-1 and 35mm f/2 at 1/250 sec., AE.

60

61

With lights just coming on, big cities are spectacular sights. The A V-1 and 50mm f/1.4, at f/11, AE.

into the wilds, your favorite type may not be available.

A trip almost always starts with some mode of transportation. Taking a picture through the window, as from the airplane on the left, is an effective way of conveying the mood of a trip. If sightseeing is your thing, then it would be folly not to take pictures of the famous places you may never see again. And don't be

The AE-1 and 70–150mm f/4.5 zoom, 1/125 sec., AE.

Taken from below, this bird became a real Johnathan Livingston Seagull. The AE-1 and 70–150mm f/4.5 zoom, 1/125 sec., AE.

afraid to take more than one shot of a different historical site or famous building. Try different exposures and angles. Then, after you get home and have the film developed, you can sort out the good from the bad.

Different angles aren't only restricted to buildings either. For instance, if you go to the seashore, a shot like the one of the seagull above will tell the story.

Taken from below, this bird stands as a graphic symbol of where the photographer was. The same is true of the tour buses, taken with a telephoto. If you have the time, a picture like this is just as valuable as shots of the attraction you go to see.

A View out the Window Is All You Need

One thing not to forget on a trip is the view from your hotel room. Using the window as a frame, the view very often will capture the feeling of the whole area, as in the pictures below of San Francisco. Especially if you're on a whirlwind trip and don't have much time, this kind of picture could end up representing your image of the town.

The AE-1 and 50mm f/1.4, 1/125 sec., AE.

The AE-1 and 35mm f/2, 1/4 sec., AE.

Sports

The snow spraying up as the skier exercises a sudden turn makes a breathtaking scene. The AE-1 and 300mm f/4, at 1/500 sec., AE. [62]

The ways to take sports shots are almost as varied as the number of different sports. Your technique will depend on whether you are indoors or outdoors, and on whether you want to freeze the action or blur it. Sports pictures can be some of the hardest to get just perfect as the situation varies so much.

Generally speaking, you will probably want to stop the action at its peak. For this, you will need a fast shutter speed, one of at least 1/250 sec. Fast film will also be necessary as, chances are, you won't be able to get too close to the action yourself. You'll have to leave that up to your lens, which will have to be a telephoto or zoom. However, the need for precise focusing due to shallow depth of field of these lenses means that you will have to use small apertures. Unless there's

plenty of sunlight like in the picture of the skier above, exposure could be a problem. The farther away you are, too, the longer the telephoto that will be necessary, which is no problem as long as you take a tripod along. A combination of the above—fast shutter speed, fast film, tripod and small aperture for maximum depth of field— will by and large stop the action breathtakingly.

Your next task is to stop the movement at the right instant. This is easy if you have the Power Winder A, A2 or Motor Drive MA. Anticipating the climax of the action is crucial. But if you wait until it happens, you'll be too late. So start shooting somewhat before this point and, with a Power Winder or Motor Drive MA doing the winding, you can't miss.

A perfect panning shot with the AE-1 and 200mm f/4 at 1/125 sec., AE.   63

64

The 300mm f/4 was the choice for this golf shot. AE-1 at 1/500 sec., AE.

65

In surfing, the action is fast and far away which is why the 600 mm lens and 1/1000 sec.,shutter speed were used.

twisting the upper part of your body. Prefocus on the spot where you wish to release the shutter. Start following the subject shortly before this spot but don't press the shutter button until it has reached your designated place. Speeds between 1/30 and 1/125 are best as anything above that will freeze the action, anything below will cause too much blur. This technique is useful not only for giving a feeling of movement but also for isolating the subject by reducing the background and foreground to mere patches of light and color.

Besides stopping the action, you have a couple of other options. You could use a slow shutter speed to blur the action. Though it may be hard to tell what the subject is doing, this technique is, at times, a good way to give the feeling of movement. Your subject will, of course, not be very clear. To get the blur and relatively sharp focus as well, another method is panning. Though this technique is never certain, when you do succeed, a spectacular photo like that of the racing car above results. The trick is to keep the subject focused in the center of the viewfinder as you follow the movement by

Panning Hints

* Use a shutter speed of between 1/30 and 1/125 sec. depending on the subject's speed.
* Get the subject in the viewfinder and start following it when it is still far away.
* Move the camera laterally along with the subject and release the shutter at the moment you think is best.
* At that moment, the movement of the camera and shutter release should be just a bit faster than that of the subject.
* Until you become experienced enough to be able to focus while moving the camera, prefocus on the spot where you want to release the shutter.
* Continue following the subject even after the shutter is released, just like a follow-through with a tennis racket.

Sports «Continued»

With the 85—300mm f/4.5 zoom pointed up to the sky, a shutter speed of 1/1000 sec., AE, was necessary. Taken with the AE-1. 66

Another effective way of taking blurred sports pictures is "racking", which was discussed earlier. An example is that of the kayak on the right. This kind of shot can only be taken with a zoom lens as it entails changing the focal length during the exposure. Since you have to turn the zoom ring to do so, a slow shutter speed is better as it gives you more time. A tripod is also a must. The effect of the action zinging out at you, however, makes this extra bit of effort well worth while.

Of course, sports aren't only done outdoors. Indoor sports are also popular and present perfect chances for great pictures. They are also harder to take because of the dim light. Once again, you will need a medium telephoto lens (those longer than 200mm do not give large

enough maximum apertures to be of much use). And if you are able to position yourself close enough to the action, a powerful flash like the 199A will be a help. If you can't get close, pushed high-speed film is necessary, but you must make sure to use a type that fits the indoor lighting if you prefer slide film. At any rate, try to get established in a place that gives a clear view of the climax of the action. Prefocus, preset the exposure and wait for things to come your way.

Blur by means of a slow shutter speed shows the action. The AE-1 and 100-200mm f/5.6 zoom, 1/15 sec., AE.

67

It looks like the photographer got splashed but there was never any danger with the 85—300mm f/4.5 zoom on the AE-1, 1/4 sec., AE.

Sports Picture Hints

1. First learn the rules of the game you are photographing. This will enable you to follow and anticipate the action so you can wait for the decisive moment.
2. Close-ups of the participants' expressions are indispensable if you want good sports shots.
3. Don't be impatient while following the action. Wait for just the right moment and masterpiece photos will be yours.

Indoor Photography

Indoor family get-togethers are best captured with a flash. The Speedlite 155A, AE-1 and 35mm f/2 lens, f/2.8 auto aperture.

Indoor photography offers the opportunity of experimenting with all sorts of different light. The natural light of mid-day, the tungsten and fluorescent light of evening, light from Speedlites and floodlamps and even candle light or Christmas tree lights. Since most parties and celebrations take place indoors, you should try to

The Speedlite 155A, AE-1 and 50mm lens at auto aperture of f/5.6.

master the art of indoor picture-taking. Actually, if you have understood the techniques we have already discussed, you will have no problem.

A Speedlite: Indoor Sun

Color negative film and daylight slide film are perfect for flash photography because the light from a Speedlite or other flash unit is closest to that of the sun. Another merit of using a flash unit is that it has a flash duration of from 1/500 sec. to 1/50,000 sec., which is fast enough to stop even the most momentary of action. You will find that lenses having focal lengths of from 35mm to 100mm are the easiest to use with Speedlites. The best combination, however, would be the 28–50 mm or 35–70mm zoom with an electronic Speedlite. The extra mobility provided by this equipment comes in handy in tight indoor situations.

Natural light through a window provides a feeling of warmth. The AE-1 and 35mm f/2, 1/60 sec., AE. 70

With Speedlite 155A at the ready, such intimate moments under dim indoor lighting are preserved forever. The AE-1 and 50mm f/1.8 lens at f/5.6. 68

A Speedlite provides light and stops action, too. The AE-1, 155A and 50mm f/1.8 lens, auto aperture of f/5.6. 69

Utilizing the Existing Light

For birthdays, holidays and family reunions, there's nothing like taking pictures using only the available natural light. It can be the sun streaming through the window, the warmth of tungsten lightbulbs, the yellow glow of candles from a birthday cake or the multi-colored lights on the Christmas tree. To get such shots, you will need high-speed film and a lens having a large maximum aperture such as f/1.2 to f/2. Under regular home lights, you may even be able to hand hold the camera. For candles or Christmas tree lights, however a tripod is a definite must, along with slow shutter speeds. In fact, B (BULB) will probably be necessary, in which case you will have to guess at the exposure. Again, experience is the key. Bracket by taking several of the same picture at different exposures and keep records of the results.

Points to Consider in Flash Photography

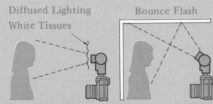

Diffused Lighting
White Tissues

Bounce Flash

● **Be careful of Shadows**
Remember that a direct frontal flash shot of a person will create small, dark shadows if a wall or another flat background is right behind; light shadows if the wall is far away. Using the Canon Synchro Cord A and an extension cord to remove the Speedlite from the camera and holding the flash at an angle eliminates such shadows.

● **Be Careful of Reflections**
If there is some sort of glass, a window for instance, in your background, harsh reflections will be captured on film. The same is true of a frontal shot of a person wearing glasses. To avoid this, change your own angle or take the Speedlite off the camera.

● **Bounce Flash**
Another way to soften the harshness and shadows caused by direct frontal lighting is to bounce the flash off a ceiling or wall. Since this technique will only give about 1/4 of the normal amount of light, however, the Speedlite's electronics may not give perfect exposure. Bracketing and experimentation are recommended. Also, make sure the ceiling or wall you use is colored white or some variation thereof. Otherwise, your subject will become tainted with that non-white color.

● **Diffused Lighting**
You can also get soft lighting by using a Wide Adapter or putting a piece of gauze cloth or several white tissues over the flash unit. If you try covering an automatic flash such as a Canon Speedlite, be careful not to cover up the unit's light sensor.

Wildlife and Pets

Coming in for a landing, this snowy heron was captured by the 800mm f/5.6 lens at 1/250 sec., AE.

71

A picture of an animal in its natural habitat shows mother nature in all her serenity and awesomeness. Birds, woodchucks, skunks, lions, elephants, you can be an animal photographer at the zoo, in a forest, or on a safari. Even your backyard will provide a good setting for photographing less wild creatures like the family cat. Where you are, of course, makes a great deal of difference on the kind of equipment you use.

Your cat or dog may be fairly easy to get on film as they are used to you and are more willing to stand still. Even at that, you can't spend a great deal of time fiddling around with the camera controls before they get tired. Of course, you could leave some food at a particular spot to entice the pet to sit still. Your best bet, though, would be to use a Speedlite and either of

the Power Winders or Motor Drive MA. The kind of lens isn't so important as long as you keep in mind that the longer the focal length, the less mobility you have.

Where a telephoto lens is a definite must is when photographing wildlife. Most of these animals are too skittish to allow you to get too close, and some are outright dangerous. Lenses above 200mm are necessary and since they have small maximum apertures, high-speed film may also be handy. Even if you have these things and a Power Winder or Motor Drive MA, however, you may still have trouble keeping up with an animal's movements. The best thing to do is study your subject's activities as much as possible beforehand. As with many kinds of photography, if you can anticipate the movements of the subject, the decisive moment will

A zoom once again gives perfect framing of this ostrich. The 85—300mm f/4.5 zoom and AE-1, 1/125 sec., AE.

Because of the 80-200mm f/4 zoom, this raccoon was unaware of the photographer's presence.

A flamingo, taken with the 70—150mm zoom and AE-1, 1/250 sec., AE.

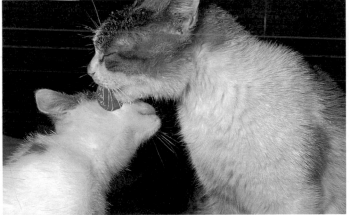

Even the household cats have their tender moments. The Speedlite 177A and 50mm f/1.8 lens, AE-1.

not be missed. Another piece of equipment you might consider is a remote control unit that is used with a motor drive. With such an accessory, you can set up your camera on a tripod at a place where an animal will appear. Then, while hiding, you can trip the shutter. If you own an A-1 or AE-1 PROGRAM and Motor Drive MA, this operation is possible by means of the Wireless Controller LC-1 or Remote Switch 60 or 3.

Getting this frog on film was tricky business. The Macro 100mm f/4, AE-1 and flash allowed the photographer to stand far enough away.

To keep as far away from the king of beasts as possible, the 500 mm f/4.5L and AE-1 were used at 1/250 sec., AE.

You don't have to take such elaborate measures in a zoo. Since the animals are penned up with nowhere to go, your most difficult task is to find the best angle and eliminate as many manifestations of captivity as possible. If you're confronted, for example, with a glass enclosure, you could use a polarizing filter to eliminate glare. Or, if the animal is behind a wire fence, you can (if allowed) put your lens right against the fence. Although this will serve to make the wires less visible, they still may bother the picture. It is therefore best to avoid that sort of situation.

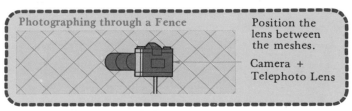

Photographing through a Fence

Position the lens between the meshes.

Camera + Telephoto Lens

Festivals

With a bit of distortion, the 17mm f/4 lens captures the flavor of this Mexican festival. The AE-1 at 1/250 sec., AE. 74

Festivals are some of the most indigenous events in a country. They are like a storybook of the history and spirit of a people. And even if you are not a worldwide traveller, the color and pageantry of the festival or parade near your locality are photographic themes not to be missed.

To get good pictures of these events, though, you may have to go to some trouble. First of all, you can't be lazy. Since festivals are heavily attended by the local populace, you will have to go very early to beat the rush. Failure to do so will mean that you'll have trouble getting shots without someone's head interfering. Then, you'll have to set yourself up in an advantageous posi-

tion to get the pictures you want. If you can get up in a tree there won't be any problem getting unobstructed pictures. Taking a step ladder along could serve the same purpose. The catch is, you have to know where the main action is going to take place. To this end, you should talk with the people in charge and find out as much as you can about times, places and routes. In some special circumstances, you may even need to get their permission.

As for equipment, a wide variety of lenses —wide-angle, standard, telephoto— are necessary. Because taking along too much equipment will limit your mobility, however, a zoom lens or two would be best. And

An upward angle with the 100mm f/2.8 puts the length of this parade in proper perspective. The AE-1 at 1/125 sec., AE.

A wide-angle lens and bird's-eye view are necessary to fit in the crush of people at a Japanese festival. The AE-1 35mm f/2 at 1/250 sec., AE.

if you strap two cameras around your neck with one zoom attached to each, you won't have to waste time changing film and lenses. Film is of course something you should prepare, and lots of it. Especially if you use either of the Power Winders or the Motor Drive MA, you will need to have a plentiful stock on hand. A Speedlite will also be indispensable if the festival continues on into the night.

Pay Attention to the Event's Surroundings

Don't forget that festivals are participatory events. To completely capture the mood of the day, you should include the faces of the onlookers and other shots of the surroundings. Moreover, don't be hesitant about moving around to get different angles, for instance a parade head on, from the side or from the back.

Close-Up Photography

(Above) The AE-1 and New Macro FD 100mm f/4.
(Below) The New Macro FD 50mm f/3.5 and Extension Tube FD25-U set-up.

The Close-up Lens 240 on the FD 100mm f/2.8 taken with the AV-1 at f/5.6, AE, made sure the butterfly didn't get away. 0.3X. 79

Previously, we've talked about why special equipment is necessary for close-up photography. It's because lenses do not magnify the subject but rather reduce its size to less than life-size. Therefore, all regular lenses have limits to how close they can get to a subject. Attempts to move in closer than this limit will result in unclear pictures. Depending on how close you wish to get, this kind of picture can be either extremely easy or fairly involved. These two pages are devoted to close-up photography (that of life-size or smaller). After that, the more complex photomacrography (greater than life-size magnifications) will be discussed.

First, it might help to know what is meant by "magnification". It is the image's height on the film divided by the height of the subject. Since you know that a picture frame is 24 x 36mm, take the vertical measure —24mm— and divide by the height of the subject. For instance, if a flower is 30mm high, you will get $\frac{24mm}{30mm}$ = 0.8X. At a magnification of 0.8X, therefore, the flower will fill up the picture frame.

Since the magnifications involved in close-up photography are not great, not much equipment is needed. Simplest is the close-up lens. Called a lens, it is more like a filter as it screws into the lens' filter threads. Canon has two close-up lenses —the 450 and 240— that can be used on any Canon lens from 35mm to 135mm. As you can see from the table below, maximum magnifications of 0.48X and 0.78X are possible respectively when used on the 135mm f/2.8 lens. Although magni-

Data for Canon Close-up Lenses

Lens	Close-up Lens 450			Close-up Lens 240		
	Minimum Shooting Distance (mm)	Field of View (mm)	Magnification	Minimum Shooting Distance (mm)	Field of View (mm)	Magnification
FD 35mm f/2	243	98x147	0.25X	215	77x116	0.31X
FD 35mm f/2.8	240	99x149	0.24X	211	78x117	0.3X
FD 50mm f/1.4	300	92.6x139	0.26X	246	67x100	0.36X
FD 50mm f/1.8	334	109x164	0.22X	259	75x112	0.32X
FD 55mm f/1.2	345	104x156	0.23X	270	71x107	0.34X
FD 85mm f/1.8	397	74x111	0.32X	300	48x72	0.5X
FD 100mm f/2.8	419	64x96	0.37X	310	41x61	0.6X
FD 135mm f/2.8	474	50x75	0.48X	350	31x46	0.78X
FD 135mm f/3.5	480	51x77	0.47X	356	31x47	0.77X

Note: Field-of-view data are based on rounded off magnifications. When calculating, there will be differences of 2~3%.

A group of praying mantises [80] *magnified 0.5X by the Macro 100 mm f/4 on the A V-1 at f/11, AE.*

This is what a seat cover looks like magnified 0.8X. The Macro 50mm + FD25-U and AE-1, 1/30 sec., AE.

A Chinese bellflower, life-size. The A V-1 and Macro 100mm f/4 + FD50-U, at f/16, AE.

fications with these lenses are not so great, they give acceptably sharp images as can be seen in the picture of the butterfly on the previous page. Also, they do not cause any loss in the speed of the primary lens.

For magnifications one step above those possible with close-up lenses, Canon offers several sets of "extension tubes". These are accessories that fit in between the camera body and lens. Since the FD-U Extension Tubes are automatic (meaning that the AE function of your A series camera will be unaffected), let's consider only this set right now. It contains three tubes of 15, 25 and 50mm, all of which can be used with any lens from 35 to 200mm (except for FD 85mm f/1.2L and FD 55mm f/1.2 ASPHERICAL). And the 15mm can be used on a 28mm lens as well. To find the magnification you would get with a particular lens, divide the tube length by the focal length of that lens. Life-size magnification (where the image and object are of equal size) is therefore possible by using the Extension Tube FD 50-U with a standard 50mm lens.

This rule doesn't work, however, with Canon's two Macro lenses. The New Macro FD 50mm f/3.5 and New Macro FD 100mm f/4 are especially corrected for aberrations to give clear images at close distances. In contrast to using close-up lenses or extension tubes on regular lenses, they allow you to get very close to the subject — 23cm and 45cm from the camera's film plane respectively, with no loss in image quality even at maximum aperture. Used by themselves, they give 0.5X magnification; used with the Extension Tube FD 25-U (for the 50mm) and FD 50-U (for the 100mm) life-size magnification is possible. And it should be noted that while both lenses render the same magnifications, the 100mm enables you to stand farther away, an advantageous feature for close-up shots of flighty insects. No matter which one you use, though, Macro lenses are ideal for close-ups, photomacrography (see next page) and copying (see pages 132-133) as well as for regular photography. Such versatility is due to their ability to continuously focus from infinity to the minimum focusing distance.

Another simple way to get close-up pictures is to use the close-focusing function available on two of Canon's zoom lenses. The New FD 35—70mm f/2.8—3.5 and New FD 28—50mm f/3.5 will give you about 0.2X magnification, convenient for hand-held shots of insects and flowers. Image quality, of course, is not comparable to what is possible with close-up lenses, extension tubes or a Macro lens.

Photomacrography

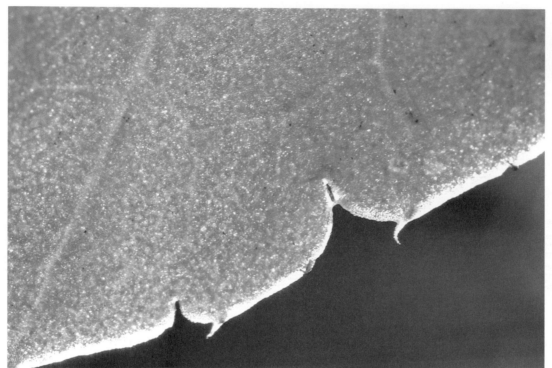

Typical Photomacrographic Set-up: Macrophoto 35mm f/2.8, Macrophoto Lens Adapter, Bellows FL and AE-1.

A begonia leaf magnified 3X with the Macrophoto Lens 35mm f/2.8, Bellows FL and AE-1, 1/125 sec., at f/8.

The main piece of equipment for photomacrography is a bellows which, as the name implies, is a flexible accordion-like device to which a lens and camera body are attached. It allows greater magnifications than would ordinarily be possible and also intermediate magnifications. Canon has three such units, with the most recent and versatile being the Auto Bellows. By attaching regular, non-macro lenses to this accessory, magnifications up to 3.4X are possible. The bellows also allows you to mount many lenses in reverse. Since lenses are designed to reduce the subject size on the film, anything over life-size presents a bit of an image quality problem. Reversal of the lens is therefore recommended for photomacrographic magnifications. You can do this trick with lenses from 28mm to 135 mm as well as with other lenses, though these others will not give larger than life-size magnifications. The chart on the right shows the magnifications possible with different lens/Auto Bellows combinations (figures for lens reversal are in parentheses). Of course, for really sharp images, you should use the Macro lenses as they give better edge-to-edge sharpness than regular lenses.

You can get even greater magnifications by using one of the two lenses that are especially for the bellows. Although these lenses, the Macrophoto 20mm f/3.5 and 35mm f/2.8, are incredibly small, they are very powerful giving up to 10.72X and 5.84X magnifications respectively.

Lens	Magnification Range
Macro FD 50mm f/3.5	0.8X–3.4X (1.3X–3.4X)
FD 50mm f/1.8	0.8X–3.4X (1.1X–3.6X)
FD 50mm f/1.4	0.8X–3.4X (1.2X–3.7X)
FD 55mm f/1.2	0.7X–3.2X
FD 85mm f/1.8	0.5X–2.1X
Macro FD 100mm f/4	0.4X–1.7X
FD 100mm f/2.8	0.4X–1.7X
FD 135mm f/2.8	0.3X–1.3X
FD 135mm f/3.5	0.3X–1.3X

Magnification Table for Auto Bellows with normally mounted lens focused at ∞ (data in parentheses for reverse-mounted lens).

Now that you know a little about some of the tools available for this kind of photography, it is time to consider some of the problems you'll run into when actually taking the picture.

There are basically two ways to approach photo-

A spider's web after the rain. The AE-1, Macro 100mm f/4 and Auto Bellows, 1/125 sec., f/11, 1.5X.

Not much of this begonia flower is in focus at 2.5X. Taken with the Macro 100mm f/4, Bellows FL and AE-1.

Here's what a blood-sucking mosquito looks like at 6X. The AE-1, Macrophoto lens 35mm f/2.8 and Bellows FL.

macrography. One is a scientific way, to be used when you want to photograph at a certain magnification, which involves complex calculations (all pertinent data can be found in Canon instruction booklets). Most photographers, though, prefer the more haphazard method of simply adjusting the bellows extension until the subject is the desired size in the viewfinder. Precise focusing can then be done with another knob without changing the magnification. Since depth of field is extremely shallow at such close distances, focusing must be exact. A little bit off and chances are the part you wish to magnify will become totally out of focus. That is why you must always use a small aperture. Exposure could then become a problem, compounded by diminished light reaching the film because of in-between accessories. Slow shutter speeds are always possible, but you have to make sure the subject and camera are absolutely still as any slight movement will be magnified. A tripod is a must. And, if you're outside, you should try and construct a make-shift wind screen around the subject. For really high magnifications, however, indoors is the safest place.

Something else you must do with the AE-1 exposure-wise is stopped-down metering. Because most close-up and photomacrographic accessories (except for the Extension Tubes FD-U) do not have automatic exposure couplings, you have to take the lens' aperture ring off "A" to a small aperture setting of your choice, push in the stop-down lever and then set the shutter speed so that the needle in the viewfinder is even with the index mark. (Caution: if you are using a New FD Lens, you must attach the Manual Diaphragm Adapter between the lens and camera body to do this procedure.) With the AV-1, the shutter speed will be automatically set even when you manually stop down the lens as above (there is no stop-down lever to worry about though, again, the Manual Diaphragm Adapter must be used for New FD lenses). This is known as stopped-down AE and is also possible with the A-1, though the stop-down lever must be pushed in.

Photomacrography is a very exciting branch of photography. To truly master it, much time, patience and study are needed. It is recommended that you purchase any of a number of books now on the market devoted to this subject. The prizes awaiting you in this normally unseen world will be more than worth the effort.

Copying

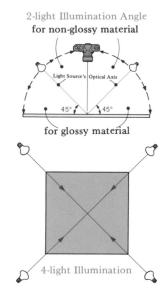

A collection of Japanese stamps taken with the AE-1 and Macro 50mm, 1/8 sec., AE.

2-light Illumination Angle
for non-glossy material

Light Source's Optical Axis

45° 45°

for glossy material

4-light Illumination

Perhaps you have never thought about it, but copying —taking pictures of flat objects such as books and stamps— is a whole photographic field in its own right. The magnifications involved range from general photography all the way to photomacrography. And of course, Canon has all the accessories necessary for doing copywork.

First, a copy stand is needed and Canon has three to offer. Such a stand is a must in order to keep the printed material perfectly flat and therefore parallel with the film. Also, it keeps both subject and camera perfectly steady, something that is also facilitated by use of a cable release for the shutter (so you don't have to touch the camera). As for lenses, the 50mm Macro and standard 50mm f/1.4 or f/1.8 are best for material of B4 size (approx. 10" x 14") or smaller. Of these, since the Macro lens is designed for close-up work, it would be better for the edge-to-edge sharpness not obtainable with a regular lens. If you want even bigger magnifications, extension tubes and a bellows could also be used.

As with close-up photography, focusing and lighting are very crucial in copywork. Because the camera is attached to the center part of the copy stand facing

downwards, you may find it helps matters to employ a Canon Angle Finder for looking in the viewfinder. Focusing should be done, not with the central split-image part of the viewfinder, but with the surrounding matte and small apertures should be used to ensure the whole thing gets into focus.

For lighting, you can set up either one, two, or four special lights above the subject. They should be positioned to strike the copy material diagonally to avoid

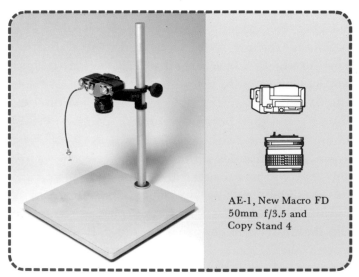

AE-1, New Macro FD
50mm f/3.5 and
Copy Stand 4

reflections. Even lighting is also very important. When using one light, put a piece of tracing paper over the light to soften it. If you have two lights, on the other hand, set them at a 45° angle or more to the material if it is not glossy, under 45° if it is. But if the material you wish to copy is rather large, using four lights should be considered.

One last thing you may find tricky is exposure. If the subject is black lettering on a white background material, your camera will expose for the white and underexposure will result. For the opposite situation —light lettering on a dark background— you will get overexposure. Keep this in mind and either increase or decrease the exposure as the case may be.

The Magnification Range of Each Photographic Field and the Lens/Accessory Combinations that Attain Them

The chart below can be used to select Canon close-up equipment for certain magnifications. Since some of these accessories have not been previously introduced in this book, you can find out more about them by obtaining the pertinent Canon brochures from your local camera dealer.

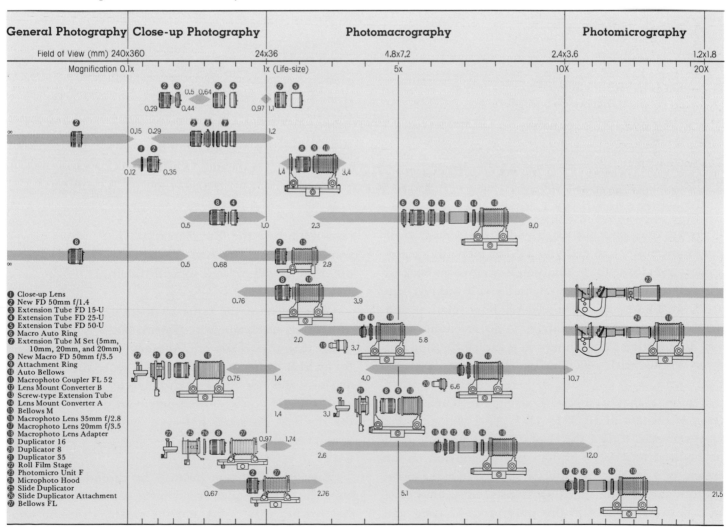

General Photography	Close-up Photography	Photomacrography	Photomicrography
Field of View (mm) 240x360	24x36	4.8x7.2	2.4x3.6	1.2x1.8
Magnification 0.1x	1x (Life-size)	5x	10X	20X

❶ Close-up Lens
❷ New FD 50mm f/1.4
❸ Extension Tube FD 15-U
❹ Extension Tube FD 25-U
❺ Extension Tube FD 50-U
❻ Macro Auto Ring
❼ Extension Tube M Set (5mm, 10mm, 20mm, and 20mm)
❽ New Macro FD 50mm f/3.5
❾ Attachment Ring
❿ Auto Bellows
⓫ Macrophoto Coupler FL 52
⓬ Lens Mount Converter B
⓭ Screw-type Extension Tube
⓮ Lens Mount Converter A
⓯ Bellows M
⓰ Macrophoto Lens 35mm f/2.8
⓱ Macrophoto Lens 20mm f/3.5
⓲ Macrophoto Lens Adapter
⓳ Duplicator 16
⓴ Duplicator 8
㉑ Duplicator 35
㉒ Roll Film Stage
㉓ Photomicro Unit F
㉔ Microphoto Hood
㉕ Slide Duplicator
㉖ Slide Duplicator Attachment
㉗ Bellows FL

Underwater Photography

3—5m below the surface, the AE-1, Marine Capsule A and flash at 1/60 sec. 81

As anyone who has experienced the sensation of being underwater can tell you, it's an incredibly variegated world down there that you'll want to go back to time and again. Not only that, but you'll want to capture it on film to show those landlubber relatives and friends of yours. Unfortunately, to do so entails more than just putting your camera in a special housing and taking it down with you. But first things first.

Canon makes a special housing for scuba divers who are owners of its A-1, AE-1, AE-1 PROGRAM and AT-1 cameras. Called the Canon Marine Capsule A, it can be used to a depth of 60m and has controls on the outside that let you manipulate shutter release, focus, aperture and shutter speed. Obviously, since your camera is entirely encased in this waterproof housing, you cannot advance the film manually. That's why a power winder must be attached. Though this is no problem, other things will present some difficulties.

One concerns the sense of depth perception, yours as well as the camera's. Objects underwater appear closer than they really are. Actually, this is no problem for an SLR owner as the distance is set to this apparent distance and not the real distance by looking in the viewfinder. If you would happen to set the focusing ring for the real distance, however, out-of-focus pictures would result.

Another thing you have to be careful of is exposure. The farther you descend in the water, the less light that reaches that point and the greater exposure you

15m below with the AE-1, Marine Capsule A and flash, 1/60 sec., f/22.   82

The AE-1, Marine Capsule   83
A and 50mm f/1.4 at 1/60
sec., AE, 15m below.   84

The AE-1, Marine Capsule A,
flash and 50mm f/1.4 at f/4.

must give. Weather and water conditions are also a factor but generally, with bright mid-day sun, clear water and calm weather, the exposure must be increased 1-1/2, 2, 2-1/2, 3 and 4 f-stops respectively at just under the surface, 6ft., 20ft., 30ft., and 50ft. below. With your A-1, AE-1, or AE 1 PROGRAM , though, you don't really have to worry about this as exposure is automatic. To save time, set the shutter speed on land, and the camera will change the aperture to suit the conditions underwater (AT-1 excepted). A shutter speed of at least 1/60 second should be used as it is difficult to hold a camera still in the ocean depths. Since this fast a shutter speed may cause exposure problems in the underwater darkness, high-speed film and an underwater flash unit may be necessary.

In fact, an underwater flash unit would be a good accessory to take along anyway as it can add the red end of the spectrum that basically disappears over 10ft. deep. Unless you like totally blue-green pictures, use one and stay within 8ft. of the subject for best color.

Canon Marine Capsule A

- Usable with Canon A-1, AE-1, AE-1 PROGRAM or AT-1 with Power Winder A attached.
- Except for zoom lenses can accept a total of 16 new and old FD lenses.
- Usable as deep as 60m (approx. 200ft.) below the surface.
- Special controls for shutter release (with lock mechanism), focusing, aperture and shutter speed.
- Allows use of two underwater flash units at same time.
- Size: φ 226mm x 195mm, Weight: 5.8kg. (Underwater weight: 1 kg.)

Astrophotography

The moon, taken with the AE-1, FL 1200mm f/11 and 2X-A Extender at 1/60 sec., effective aperture f/22., ASA 160 film was push-processed to 640. [85]

Become tired of earthly photographic pursuits? You might then think of turning your camera up to the sky. There are a myriad things to catch on film there: the sun, the moon, the planets, the stars.

You can take pictures of the heavens in two basic ways. Either affix your camera to a tripod and take long exposures or use the camera with a telescope and pursue the stars by manually moving the whole set-up. For the former method, the faster the lens and film speed, the better.

When you wish to photograph the stars so they appear as you see them, you should mount the camera on a tripod, find the star constellation you want in the viewfinder and focus at infinity. Although you should use as big an aperture as possible, f/2.8 or smaller is recommended to ensure sharpness. Any lens could be used, depending on how much of the sky you wish to get on film. Exposure varies with the brightness of the sky and film sensitivity. Between 1/8 and 1/15 is the slowest you can use without the movement of the stars creating streaks. Since you are shooting at night, high-speed film is of course necessary, and it will probably need to be push-processed.

On the other hand, if the movement of the stars is your aim (or more precisely the apparent movement caused by the rotation of the earth), you will need really long exposures of from several minutes to hours.

Star tracks. The AE-1 and 50mm f/1.4, 15 min. on the B setting.

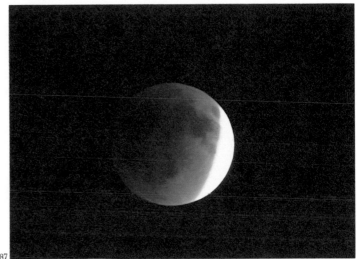

A different shot of the moon with the FL 1200mm and AE-1. 1/250 sec., f/11 and ASA 400 film.

The closer to the North Pole you are, the more curved the star tracks will be. On the equator, they will appear as straight lines. You may want to prepare a piece of cardboard or wood covered with black material. Place it in front of the lens when releasing the shutter and any vibration caused by release will not show up on the film. Because of the long exposures required, you will find that your camera's battery gets weak. Carry a spare or use the External Battery Pack A (AV-1 excluded) for an extra power boost. Also, if you live in a big city, it would be best to take a ride out to the country and set up your equipment as the lights of the city could present an exposure problem.

You may also want to photograph the sun or moon. If so, keep in mind that the image on the film will be only 1/100 the focal length (with a 50mm lens, a mere 0.5mm). A 200mm lens is just about right to emphasize the sun or moon and their immediate surroundings. Anything shorter and they will be lost in the vastness of the universe. As far as shutter speed is concerned, the moon is brighter than the stars so such slow shutter speeds as mentioned previously are not necessary. The sun, however, presents a different problem as you have to decrease its brightness by using an ND/R filter combination and low-sensitivity film. You should also take care not to look through the viewfinder with your

naked eye when using a telephoto lens to which the above filters are not attached. The increased brightness of the sun could possibly harm that organ.

Regardless of your astrophotographic method, AE photography will not usually be possible due to the dark conditions. Bracketing and lots of experience will therefore be necessary before you become successful.

Astrophotography is just one way you can combine your photographic artistry with a scientific pursuit.

Manual Telescope Guidance Set-up
By the aforementioned techniques, you cannot photograph stars of low magnitude. Use of a refraction, equatorial telescope will enable this. On top of the telescope's lens barrel, affix the camera so that its lens' optical axis is parallel to the optical axis of the telescope. Following the movement of the stars with this set-up and using a long exposure time will give you beautiful pictures even of stars with magnitudes of 8 or 9.

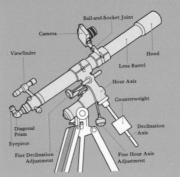

Travel Modes

BART, as it's waiting to leave Oakland West Station. The AE-1 and FD 50mm f/1.4 lens at 1/250 sec., AE. 88

Modes of transportation come in all shapes and sizes. From the rickshaw that can still be found in some parts of Asia to good old AMTRAK and the family car, pictures of the local vehicles can take the place of hundreds of words for describing a particular scene. Even a trip to your local airport provides a good picture-taking opportunity.

The kind of lenses you use will make a great deal of difference in the type of picture you get. Take your car, for example. For an ordinary picture, a standard lens would suffice. For something out of the ordinary, however, use a wide-angle or super-wide-angle and get close. The hood will appear huge and lots of background will be included. Likewise, when you go to an airport, a long zoom would be handy as it enables you to get an overall view, a select view of one airplane, or a close-up of a window or engine. If you are outside, a shot of an airplane taking off against a background of blue sky is always effective. Just be careful of possible backlight problems. You may even want to underexpose the picture a bit by pushing the film or by using a polarizer to make the sky bluer. This filter will also be handy to eliminate glare from the window if you're taking pictures from inside the waiting lounge.

Trains, too, make interesting subjects. If you live or happen to be out West, it is possible to photograph mile-long freight trains as there is nothing to block your view. In the city as well, indoor shots of train stations or subway platforms are very effective. To avoid drawing attention to yourself, take along a lens having a large

The 20mm lens gives an unusual view from this passenger ship. The AE-1 at 1/125 sec., AE. ASA 25 film.

An electric bus heading for the suburbs of San Francisco. The AE-1 and 50mm f/1.4 at 1/250 sec., AE. 90

◄ *San Francisco's famous cable car taken with the AE-1 and 200mm, 1/250 sec., AE.*

89

91

Air shows are great picture-taking events. The AE-1 and 35mm f/2, 1/250 sec., AE.

maximum aperture and high-speed film. That way, you may not need a flash. And if you're a passenger on some form of mass transit, you can get good candids of your fellow commuters by prefocusing, setting the shutter speed to what you guess will give proper exposure, resting the camera on your lap and surreptitiously pressing the shutter button (assuming that you can sit down, of course).

As with all other kinds of photography, pictures of transportation are what you make them. They can be either common-place or eye-catching. Use of the techniques and accessories that we have previously discussed will ensure the latter result.

Interiors of Transportation are Interesting, too
Who knows what these two curious train riders have discovered. Although a type of candid photography, you shouldn't forget the people who ride in 92 modes of travel. They can be even more interesting than the machine. But since they may not like you taking their picture or will pose if they know what you're up to, a good technique is to prefocus (guess the distance and set the focusing ring to that distance), put the camera on your lap, pick a shutter speed (AE-1 / AE-1 PROGRAM) or aperture (AV-1) and nonchalantly push the shutter button. Obviously, a wide-angle lens will be handy for this trick.

Still Lifes

Even your plate and silverware are good still life subjects. The Macro 50mm f/3.5 and AE-1, 1/2 sec., AE.

93

A still life can be almost any object that doesn't move. A product such as a stove or some plates. A pot of flowers. Some fruit. This genre has been a favorite of painters for centuries as it affords total freedom in arranging light, color and composition. For these same reasons it is a popular form of photography as well.

One of the most important things for still lifes is composition. Everything in the picture, background included, should be there to enhance the main theme. It is not really effective to put a hodgepodge of things together; pick and arrange things that are related to each other. You still have a lot of composition possibilities, as the theme can change depending on the combination of things. For instance, a still life of a pen and

calculator conveys a different story than that of a pen and some stationery.

The background also must be arranged to fit the subject. Besides employing special tables or stands, you can also buy what is known as seamless background paper. Rolled up and standing on legs so it can be pulled down just like a slide screen, this paper comes in all sorts of different colors and patterns. Choose the kind that is most in harmony with your theme.

There are several tricks to really creative still lifes. One is lighting. Remember the basics of lighting and arrange photolamp(s) to get the effect you want. For instance, you can soften the light to give deeper colors

A good advertisement for a restaurant, thanks to the Macro 100mm and AV-1, f/11, AE.

Models of ancient guns taken with the Macro 100mm on the A-1 at f/16, stopped-down AE.

or silhouette the subject with backlighting. On the other hand, sidelighting will emphasize the shape of the still life. And natural lighting will give a fresh, life-like feeling, which can be enhanced by giving the subject (especially if it is fruit or vegetables) a squirt with a spray bottle.

Since photolamps are, in many cases, required for really good still lifes, this kind of picture is often taken in a studio type of environment. So that you don't get in the way of your lighting, a short telephoto from 85 mm to 135mm is necessary. Any focal length shorter will limit your lighting possibilities and a wide-angle will cause distortion. Close-up equipment may also come in handy as your subject will often be rather small and you will want as sharp an image as possible. For that reason, all of the pictures on these two pages were taken with the Macro 50mm or 100mm lenses. Film-wise, low ASAs like 25 or 64 are recommended for their added sharpness. A tripod would thus be good security against camera movement as would a cable release (your camera's self-timer can be used in place of a cable release).

Other equipment you may need include a polarizer to soften reflections and the Angle Finder B.This latter accessory lets you look into the viewfinder when the camera is in a postion that normally would not enable you to do so. It is especially useful when looking directly down on a subject.

Still lifes are some of the easiest pictures to get subjects for as almost everything that you use or eat daily is a candidate. With a little care in composition and lighting you will soon be getting still life photos that would make Cézanne envious.

Now that you have learned almost all there is to know about photography, you have probably collected quite a few pictures as a result of your trial and error. Regardless of whether you take slides or prints, storing them and keeping them in some semblance of order could present quite a dilemma. Before you know it, you will have an overflow situation. To control this explosion, one thing you can do is periodically purge your collection of bad or repetitious photos. Be merciless. Keep only those that most represent your photographic skill or that have some sentimental value. Once you have done this, your next task is to store them.

As far as prints are concerned, putting them in an album under protective plastic pages is popular as this makes them easy to show and tells a story. You could also put individual prints in special acid-free envelopes and write on the outside the subject matter and date. Some of your better prints, however, demand special attention. Enlarging these pictures and mounting them is a creative display technique. Enlarging can be done at any photo dealer and either you or a custom frame-maker can mount them. Usable mounting materials range from normal wooden picture frames to cardboard, plastic and foam board. If you decide to use a plain backing without a frame, you could either let one of these materials be larger than the picture or mount the print flush with the backing. Either way you do it, such a display kills two birds with one stone. It shows off your picture-taking expertise and is a good home decoration scheme besides.

If you work with prints a lot, you may find the negatives a bit of a nuisance. They should be kept, however, as you never know when you may want to enlarge or get an extra of some picture. Negatives can be kept in a special binder inside plastic sleeves. Make sure that each strip is separate lest they end up scratching each other.

If you take slides, you will find plastic sheets with individual spaces for 20 very handy. Fill up one sheet with a certain theme and label the pictures by subject or date so they will be easy to find the next time you wish to show them. Often-handled slides can be put separately in plastic sleeves upon which you can also write pertinent data. This will protect them from dust and finger prints. You yourself can go a long way to that end as well by handling pictures (slides and prints) only by the edges. Other ways of storing slides are keeping them in the box that comes back from the processors or in the slide tray you use for your slide show (and keep the tray in its box).

The term "slide show" may sound a bit highfalutin but it's the only way to show your slides to others. Actually, it can be either one slide at a time manually inserted into the projector, a whole tray or cube of slides prepared in logical order beforehand or a bank of projectors synchronized by a computer and accompanied by a sound track from a tape deck. No matter how sophisticated you wish to be, organization and pace are important factors. You have to arrange your slides in a manner that captures the audience's attention. They should be grouped by subject with a transition in between, if possible. To help you do this, a handy device is a light table, either a ready-made one that you can buy or a self-made one using a sheet of glass, tissue or tracing paper and any lamp placed underneath the glass and pointed upwards. Such a table enables you to lay out many slides at one time and arrange them in the most interesting sequence. And in making a transition from one sequence to another, you should avoid sudden changes in tone or brightness,

Touching close-ups are always 96
appreciated by the bride and groom. The
AV-1 and 135mm f/2.8 with
Softmat filter.

Don't forget the interior of the church 97
for wedding photos. The AV-1 and
50mm f/1.4, at f/8.

Sports clubs are always looking for 98
good advertising pictures. The AE-1 and
100mm f/2, 1/250 sec., AE.

Pictures are all around you and so are the photographers who take them. The occupation known as professional photography is one that has a certain aura of romanticism and excitement about it. Upon hearing of such a person, you might immediately think of photographing beautiful women (or muscular men) as a fashion photographer or of going to far-flung corners of the globe as a photo-journalist. Indeed, these are legitimate and interesting professions. But the only things such professionals have over you is this: experience, more equipment and the money they make out of their endeavors.

You, however, don't have to go to New York City or to a battlefield to become a professional. You can do it right in your own city, without needing much more than the basic equipment you already possess. And while it may not be the most glamorous work, the possibilities you have to make money from your hobby are almost endless.

Weddings

This is one of the more popular and lucrative types of photography. Not only will the bride and groom want pictures, but so will many of their friends and relatives. You will have to start small, however, as there are undoubtedly photographers already established in your town. You should therefore ask relatives or friends to appoint you as their photographer. That way, you can build up a portfolio and establish yourself as a wedding photographer.

Once you have taken the wide variety of pictures necessary, you should compile an album of them to sell to the bride, which is included in the basic charge. There are many other opportunities for additional sales of similar albums to the parents of the bride and groom and smaller albums for relatives and friends. You could even take a picture of the cake, one of the reception band or one of the interior of the church to sell to the caterer, group or church for publicity purposes. And don't forget that when the couple's first anniversary rolls around, they may want to order some photos they didn't have a chance to buy before. Mark this date on your calendar.

School Activities

Schools are busy places and present the enterprising photographer with many opportunities. They are more than just prom pictures (which are difficult to get anyway because the school usually has a contract with another photographer). Every school has loads of after-school clubs with the students doing their thing and proud of it. You could go along and get both group and individual pictures. Drama is especially good as you could take pictures not only for the actors and their parents, but for local and school newspapers as well. Be on the lookout, too, for dances and parties. If you can photograph each couple as they enter the room, lots of sales will result. Art and science exhibits by students and photos of cheerleaders are possibilities as well.

Amateur Sports and Theater

In any community, you can find many amateur sports teams and theater groups. Regardless of whether they are just out to have fun or are budding professionals, all the participants

This kind of picture could make the national news.
The AE-1 and 100—200mm f/5.6 zoom at 1/500 sec., AE.

would enjoy a picture of themselves and their fellow athletes or actors. An example of sports would be bowling. Find out from the bowling alley manager when company teams play then go that night and (with the manager's and captain's permission) shoot away. You can do the same thing with Little League baseball and Pop Warner football games and country-club golf matches. Your customers? Participants, parents and the local newspaper.

Amateur theater groups can be a real gold mine for photo sales, both present and future. There are little theater groups and summer stock companies everywhere that need individual, publicity, and newspaper photos. The latter are especially full of budding actors who may make it big in the future. If you have a stock of their pictures, who knows? Perhaps if they become famous you will be able to sell such oldies but goodies to newspapers and magazines.

For Businesses

From specialty shops and restaurants in malls to private sports and health clubs to manufacturers, most businesses are in need of publicity photos. Although bigger concerns have enough money to employ ad agencies, many smaller ones don't. That's where you can offer your services. If it's a manufacturing facility, pictures of their production line could be used for trade journals or annual reports. A retailer may appreciate pictures of his displays for advertising. Sports clubs need examples of their patrons in action for promotional brochures. You should also try to make yourself known in the annual report market. Small companies who can't afford professionals may hire you to do their report. If you do a competent job, you will probably be requested for yearly repeat performances.

Stock Photo Sales

One thing a photographer must do is establish a file system. If you keep track of all the pictures you take, they will be easy to find if you should need them. This could happen if a former client comes back wanting duplicates. Or, you could drum up business yourself by trying to sell pictures from your stock to postcard companies, calendar companies, travel magazines or for ad brochures. These places may need out-of-season photos, just like local newspapers often need winter scenes to cool down the summer and summer scenes to warm up the winter.

If you think you've got some particularly good, unusual photographs, you can also think about trying to sell them through a photo stock company. They will sell them for you and give 60% of the sale value to you for color, 50% for black-and-white. You should be prepared, though, never to see your photos again and it may take months or years before one is sold. Giving some of your work to stock companies could be quite a money-making proposition, on the other hand, if a picture is sold for a big advertising campaign. Of course, the choice is yours. With rather run-of-the-mill pictures, you will probably do better on your own.

Spot News Coverage

The best shots of the Kent State shootings were taken by curious amateurs who grabbed their cameras and ran to the scene. With that in mind, you too can become an on-the-spot news photographer by following police and fire department vehicles on their way to a call. Many times you will be the first on the scene or the newspaper photographers will arrive too late. Call these newspapers or TV stations and offer your work. Be sure to get overview shots as well as close-ups and take down the who, what, when, and where. Often, your pictures may also prove of use to the insurance companies and owners of the home, car, or whatever. And if you are really interested in news photography, you could become a "stringer", a photographer who takes news pictures in a certain small town and sends them to the near-by big city to be put on TV or in the newspaper.

As you can see, making money with your photographs is what you make of it. You could practice it on the side for pocket money or have it become your means of existence. Keep the following things in mind, be aggressive and success will be yours.
1. Charge enough to cover your costs and to make a slight profit on each picture.
2. Keep an orderly stock of pictures for all occasions.
3. Get model releases whenever possible to avoid invasion of privacy problems.
4. Distribute plenty of business cards.
5. Get the permission of owners of establishments where you want to shoot.
6. Follow, but stay well out of the way of, any rescue vehicles.
7. When your work is printed, try to get as many by-lines as possible to build up your reputation.

At first glance, camera specifications may seem so overwhelming that you don't even want to look at them. More than anything else, though, they tell the capabilities of a camera or piece of photographic equipment. Compare, for instance, the Meter Coupling Range of the A-1 and AE-1. The A-1 goes down to EV −2 whereas the AE-1 reaches its limit at EV 1. By this, you are able to tell that the former camera can meter in darker situations and is therefore probably more expensive. Comparing specifications in this way is the best method for telling exactly what you are getting for your money.

On the following pages are the complete specifications for each A series camera and accessory.

CANON AE-1

Type: 35mm SLR (Single-Lens-Reflex) camera with electronically controlled shutter-speed priority AE (Automatic Exposure) and focal plane shutter.
Usable Lenses: Canon FD series with full aperture metering and AE coupling. Canon FL series with stopped-down metering.
Field of View: 93.5% vertical and 96% horizontal coverage of the actual picture area.
Viewfinder Information: Split-image/microprism rangefinder, aperture scale with meter needle and stopped-down metering index mark doubling as battery power level check mark. Two red zones to warn of overexposure, manual aperture control "M" signal and underexposure/coupling range warning lamp.
AE Mechanism: Electronically-controlled shutter-speed priority AE metering system.
Meter Coupling Range: EV1 (1 sec. at f/1.4) to EV18 (1/1000 sec. at f/16) with ASA 100 film and FD 50mm f/1.4 lens.
Film Speed Dial: ASA 25 to ASA 3200.
Exposure Compensation: By pressing the backlight control switch, exposure is corrected by opening the diaphragm 1.5 f/stops more on the aperture scale than the actual setting.
Shutter Speeds: 1/1000 ～ 1, 2, B.
Shutter Speed Dial: The number 2 for two seconds is marked in orange; other numbers are in white. There is a shutter dial guard to prevent unintentional movement of the dial. The ASA ring is located underneath the shutter speed dial.
Self-Timer: Electronically controlled self-timer. It releases the shutter after a lag of 10 seconds. A red LED lamp revealed blinks on and off to indicate its operation.
Power Source: One 6.2V silver oxide battery (UCAR Eveready No. 544 or Mallory PX28) or alkaline manganese battery UCAR Eveready No. 537). The battery lasts approximately one year under normal use.
Flash Synchronization: X-synchronization is at 1/60 second. M synchronization is at 1/30 second and below. PC type flash terminal available.
Automatic Flash Control: With Canon Speedlite 133A, 155A, 177A and 199A.
Back Cover: With memo holder. Can be replaced by the Canon Data Back A.

Film Advance Lever: Single stroke with 120° throw and stand-off angle of 30°. Film can be wound with several short strokes.
Frame Counter: Additive type, automatically resets itself when the back cover is opened. While rewinding film, it counts the frame numbers downward.
Size: 141 × 87 × 47.5mm (5-9/16″ × 3-7/16″ × 1-7/8″) (body only)
Weight: 590g (20-13/16 ozs.) (body only) 770g (27-3/16 ozs.) with the 50mm f/1.8 standard lens.

CANON AV-1

Type: 35mm SLR (Single-Lens-Reflex) camera with electronically controlled AE (Automatic Exposure).
Usable Lenses: Canon FD (for full aperture AE) and most FL (for stopped-down AE) series lenses.
Field of View: 92% vertical and 93% horizontal coverage of the actual picture area.
Viewfinder Information: Split-image/microprism rangefinder, shutter speed scale and meter needle, red over-and underexposure warning indices, battery check/camera shake warning index.
AE Mechanism: Aperture priority AE control.
Selector Dial: Five positions: ⒜ for normal aperture priority AE and automatic flash with Canon Speedlite 133A, 155A, 177A or 199A, 60⚡ for flash photography with other flashes, A Self for self-timer aperture priority AE and self-timer flash with Canon Speedlite 133A, 155A, 177A or 199A, Self ⚡ for self-timer flash with other flashes, B (Bulb) for time exposures.
Exposure Preview: Meter needle activated by pressing the shutter button halfway.
Shutter Speed: Automatically controlled, steplessly, from 2 sec. to 1/1000 sec. Manual settings for B (Bulb) and X-synchronization speed of 1/60 sec. with flashes other than Canon Speedlite 133A, 155A, 177A or 199A.
ASA Film Speed Dial: ASA 25 to ASA 1600. With lock.
Meter Coupling Range: EV1 (f/1.4 at 1 sec.) to EV18 (f/22 at 1/500 sec.) with ASA 100 film and the FD 50mm f/1.4 lens.
Exposure Compensation: Shutter speed is automatically reduced 1-1/2 steps to increase exposure by pressing backlight control switch.
Self-timer: Electronically controlled. 10-second time lag activated by pressing shutter button. Red LED blinks to indicate operation; flashing frequency increases two sec. before shutter release. Cancellation possible.
Flash Synchronization: At 1/60 sec. Set by switching selector dial to 60 ⚡ for flashes other than the Canon Speedlite 133A, 155A, 177A or 199A. Direct contact at accessory shoe.
Automatic Flash Control: With Canon Speedlite 133A, 155A, 177A or 199A. With selector dial at ⒜.
Film Advance Lever: Single-stroke 120° throw with 30° stand-off. Winding with several short strokes possible.
Frame Counter: Additive type. Automatically resets to "S" upon opening back cover.
Power Source: One 6.2V silver oxide (UCAR Eveready No.544, Mallory PX28) or alkaline manganese (UCAR Eveready No. 537) battery.
Dimensions: 139 × 85 × 47.5mm (5-1/2″ × 3-3/8″ × 1-7/8″).
Weight: 490g (17-5/16 ozs.) body only, including battery.
670g (23-5/8 ozs.) with FD 50mm f/1.8 lens.
730g (25-3/4 ozs.) with FD 50mm f/1.4 lens.

Power Winder A, Speedlites and Macrolite ML-1 Specifications 163

Power Winder A ...Usable for: A Series Cameras
Winding Speed: About 0.5 second. **Shutter Speed Coupling Range:** 1/60 to 1/1000 second for continuous photography. "B" to 1/1000 second for single frame photography. **Mounting:** Attached via the tripod socket after the winder coupler cover has been removed. **Power Source:** Four penlight batteries (size AA); good for more than 20 rolls of 36-exposure film under normal temperatures. **Size:** 141mm (W) x 42mm (D) x 34mm (H). (5-9/16" x 1-5/8" x 1-5/16") **Weight:** 300g (10-9/16 ozs.) including batteries.

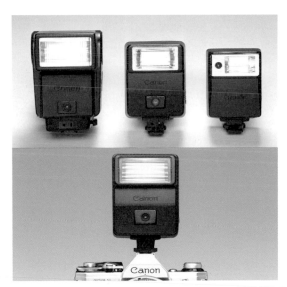

Speedlite 199A ...Usable for: A Series Cameras
Guide Number: 30 (ASA 100, m) or 50 (ASA 25, ft.). **Recycling Time:** Less than 10 sec. with penlight batteries and 0.2 - 10 sec. on automatic; less than 6 sec. with Ni-Cd batteries and 0.2 - 6 sec. on automatic. **Number of Flashes:** More than 100 with penlight batteries and 100 to 1,000 on automatic; more than 50 with Ni-Cd batteries and 50 to 500 on automatic. **Aperture Choices:** f/2.8, f/5.6 and f/11 at ASA 100. **Auto Coupling Ranges:** 1.5 m to 10.6 m at the red position (f/2.8, ASA 100) and, with wide adapters, 1.5 m to 6.3 m. At the green position, 1 m to 5.3 m (f/5.6, ASA 100) **Flash Coverage:** Adequate for 35mm lens on a 35mm format. With wide adapter, adequate coverage for 24mm lens. **Shutter Speed Selector Switch:** Automatically sets the camera's shutter speed to 1/60 when at AUTO; automatically sets speeds to 1/60 in case of shutter settings faster than 1/60; and for settings slower than 1/60, shutter will be released at the speed set on the camera, when the selector switch on the back of the flash is at the MANU/60-30S position. **Usable Film Speeds:** ASA 25 to 800. **Power Source:** Four penlight batteries. **Bounce:** Bounce feature with click stops at 90, 75, and 60 degrees. **Size:** 79mm (W) x 83mm (D) x 116mm (H). (3-1/8" x 3-1/4" x 4-1/2") **Weight:** 490g (1 lb. 1-5/16 oz.) including batteries. **Accessories:** Case, Wide Adapter, and optional Synchro Cord A.

Speedlite 177A ...Usable for: A Series Cameras
Guide Number: 25 (ASA 100, m) or 41 (ASA 25, ft.), 16 (ASA 100, m) or 26 (ASA 25, ft.) with Wide Adapter 177A. **Recycling Time:** Less than 8 sec. using alkaline-manganese batteries. Less than 6 sec. using Ni-Cd batteries. **Number of Flashes:** 200 or more using alkaline-manganese batteries. 70 or more using Ni-Cd batteries. **Flash Duration:** 1/600 sec. − 1/50,000 sec. **Aperture Selection Switch:** Three positions: f/2.8 (red), f/5.6 (green), and manual (M) at ASA 100. **Auto Shooting Distance Range:** 1.0 − 4.5m (1.0 − 5.7m with Wide Adapter 177A) at red "A". 0.5 − 4.5m (0.5 − 2.8m with Wide Adapter 177A) at green "A". **ASA Film Speed Scale:** ASA 25 to ASA 800. **Aperture Scale:** f/1 − f/32. **Distance Scale:** 0.5 − 20m (2 − 65 ft.) **Power Source:** Four penlight (AA) alkaline-manganese or Ni-Cd batteries. **Dimensions:** 72 (W) x 58 (D) x 107 (H)mm. (2-13/16" x 2-5/16" x 4-3/16"). **Weight:** 310g (10-15/16 ozs.) including batteries. **Accessories:** Soft Case, Wide Adapter 177A, Synchro Cord A (optional).

Speedlite 155A ...Usable for: A Series Cameras
Guide Number: 17 (ASA 100, m) or 28 (ASA 25, ft.). **Recycling Time:** Less than 7 sec. with alkaline batteries; or less than 5 sec. when using Ni-Cd batteries. Pilot lamp glows when flash is ready. **Number of Flashes:** More than 300 using alkaline batteries. More than 90 using Ni-Cd batteries. **Aperture Selection Switch:** Three settings: Red (f/2.8 at ASA 100), MANU., and Green (f/5.6 at ASA 100). **Auto Shooting Distance Range:** 0.5m to 6m at f/2.8 (ASA 100) 0.5m to 3m at f/5.6 (ASA 100). **Power Source:** Four AA size batteries. **Usable Film Speeds:** ASA 25 to ASA 800. **Aperture Scale:** 1 to 32. **Distance Scale:** 0.5 to 15m. **Size:** 70mm (W) x 51mm (D) x 105mm (H). (2-3/4" x 2" x 4-1/8"). **Weight:** 300g (10-9/16 ozs.) including batteries. **Accessories:** Case, and optional Synchro Cord A.

Speedlite 133A ...Usable for: A Series Cameras
Guide Number: 16 (ASA 100, m) or 26 (ASA 25, ft.). **Recycling Time:** Less than 9 sec. using alkaline-manganese batteries. Less than 6 sec. using Ni-Cd batteries. **Number of Flashes:** 100 or more using alkaline-manganese batteries. 70 or more using Ni-Cd batteries. **Flash Duration:** 1/700 sec. − 1/100,000 sec. **ASA Film Speed Switch:** Two positions: ASA 80, 100 (green), ASA 400 (orange). **Auto Shooting Distance Range:** 1.0 − 8m at orange 'A'. 0.5 − 4m at green "A". **ASA Film Speed Scale:** ASA 80 − 100 and 400. **Aperture Scale:** f/4. **Distance Scale:** 0.5 − 8m (2−26ft.). **Power Source:** Two penlight alkaline-manganese or Ni-Cd batteries. **Dimensions:** 62 (W) x 37 (D) x 95 (H)mm. (2-7/16" x 1-7/16" x 3-9/4"). **Weight:** 200g (7-1/16 ozs.) including batteries. **Accessories:** Soft Case.

Macrolite ML-1 ...Usable for: A Series Cameras with the Macro FD Lenses and FD 80−200mm f/4 + CL 500T
Guide Number: 16 (ASA 100, m); 9.5 (ASA 100, m) with Wide Adapter. **Flash Duration:** 1/500−1/50,000 sec. **Aperture Selection Switch:** Four positions. Three are color-coded auto aperture settings which differ with ASA film speed: Red (f/5.6 at ASA 100), Green (f/11 at ASA 100), Yellow (f/22 at ASA 100), and MANU. **Auto Flash Shooting Distance Range:** Red; 0.6−2.8m (2−9.3 ft.), Green; 0.4−1.4m (1.3−4.7 ft.), Yellow; 0.4−0.7m (1.3−2.3 ft.). Less with Wide Adapter. **Dimensions and Weight:** Flash Unit; 131 (W) x 39.7 (D) x 99 (H)mm (5-3/16" x 1-9/16" x 3-7/8"), 170g (6 ozs.), Control Unit; 50 (W) x 59 (D) x 38.6 (H)mm (2" x 2-1/4" x 1-1/2"), 70g (2-7/16 ozs.), Battery Case; 77.4 (W) x 35.6 (D) x 162 (H)mm (3-1/6" x 1-7/16" x 6-3/8"), 560g (1 lb. 3-3/4 ozs.) including batteries.

Data Back A ...Usable for: AE-1, A-1 and AT-1

Attachment: In place of the back cover of the A-1, AE-1 and AT-1. **Data Setting Dials:** Right dial:32 figures (0 to 31) and two blanks. Central dial: 39 figures (0 to 31; A to G) and a blank. Left dial: 39 figures (0 to 9; 79 to 90; I to X; a to g) and a blank. **Data Imprinting:** Special synchronization cord connection. The built-in lamp imprints the necessary data on the film from the back. **Power Source:** One 6V silver oxide battery (UCAR Eveready No. 544 or Mallory PX28) or alkaline battery (UCAR Eveready No. 537 or Mallory 7K13) which is good for more than 8,000 exposures. **Size:** 100mm (W) x 48.5mm (D) x 14.5mm (H). (3-15/16" x 1-15/16" x 9/16"). **Weight:** 160g (5-5/8 ozs.) including battery. **Accessories:** Special synchronization cord and case.

CANON A-1

Type: 35mm SLR (Single-Lens-Reflex) camera with electronically controlled, multiple-mode AE (automatic exposure) and focal plane shutter.
Photographic Modes: Six modes, including 5 AE modes: shutter-speed priority AE, aperture priority AE, programmed AE, full AE flash photography with specified Canon electronic flashes, and stopped-down AE, as well as manual override.
Usable Lenses: Canon FD lenses (usable with 4 full aperture metering AE modes and with stopped-down AE): Canon FL lenses (usable with stopped-down AE).
Field of View: 93.5% vertical and 95.3% horizontal coverage of the actual picture area.
Focusing Screen: Standard split-image/microprism rangefinder.
Viewfinder Information: Displayed in the form of LED digital readout below the visual field. Includes shutter speed, aperture, flashing warning of incorrect exposures and settings, bulb indication, charge completion indicator with specified Canon flash units, manual aperture control signal, error indication for incorrect stopping-down operation. Shutter speed and aperture data displayed in 1/2 step increments. Viewfinder information can be cancelled by turning off the viewfinder display switch.
AE Mechanism: Electronically controlled. Employs 3 LSIs with I²L, one Linear LSI and one Bi-MOS IC for light metering.
AE Mode Selection: By means of the AE mode selector. Two main settings: Tv for shutter-speed priority AE, Av for aperture priority AE.
ASA Film Speed Setting: ASA 6 to ASA 12800 in 1/3 step increments. With lock.

Meter Coupling Range: EV-2 to EV18 at ASA 100 with FD 50mm f/1.4 lens. In the programmed AE mode, meter coupling range depends on the programmed shutter speed and aperture combinations.
Exposure Compensation: ± 2 f/stop scale gradations in increments of 1/3 of a gradation, with 1/4, 1/2, 2, and 4 markings.
Exposure Memory: EV is stored and locked when the exposure memory switch is pressed. When pressed, the shutter-speed aperture combination can be changed for the same EV stored in the memory.
Manual Override: Possible by disengaging the FD lens from the "A" mark and setting the AE mode selector to Tv. Aperture manually controlled with aperture ring; shutter speed with AT dial.
Shutter Speed Scale: B, 30, 15, 8, 4, 2, 1, 2, 4, 8, 15, 30, 60, 125, 250, 500, 1000 plus P (with AE mode selector at Tv). "P" setting is required for programmed AE mode. Intermediate speeds not on the scale cannot be set.
Aperture Scale: 1.4 · 2 · 2.8 · 4 · 5.6 · 8 · 11 · 16 · 22 (with the AE mode selector at Av)
Power Source: One 6.2V silver oxide battery (UCAR Eveready No. 544, Mallory PX28) or alkaline manganese battery (UCAR Eveready No. 537).
Battery Check: A red LED on top of the camera flashes on and off to indicate power level when the battery check button is pressed. Flashing frequency decreases with power level.
Main Switch: 2 positions: "A" and "L". At "L" all circuits are off and the shutter button is locked as a safety feature. Doubles as self-timer lever.
Multiple Exposure: Possible by setting multiple exposure lever before winding film advance lever to recock shutter. Frame counter does not advance. Unlimited.
Self-timer: Electronically controlled. Activated by pressing shutter button. A choice of 2 or 10 seconds time lag is available. Red LED flashes on and off to indicate its operation. Flashing frequency increases 2 sec. before shutter release.
Flash Synchronization: X-synch at 1/60 sec., FP- and M-synch at 1/30 sec. and slower.
Flash Coupling: Accessory shoe has contacts for directly coupled flash units and automatic flash control contacts for automatic exposure. PC type flash terminal with shock preventive rim on front of the body.
Automatic Flash: Full AE flash photography with Canon Speedlites 133A, 155A, 177A and 199A. Shutter speed automatically set. Aperture automatically controlled according to the flash settings.
Back Cover: Opened by pulling up rewind knob. Removable for attaching Data Back A. With memo holder.
Film Advance Lever: Single-stroke 120° throw with 30° stand off. Winding with several short strokes is possible. Automatic winding possible by mounting Canon Motor Drive MA or Power Winder A.
Frame Counter: Additive type. Counts back frames as film is rewound. Automatically resets to "S" upon opening back cover. Does not advance during multiple exposure.
Size: 144 × 91.5 × 47.5mm (5-1/2" × 3-5/8" × 7/8) body only.
Weight: 620g (1 lb. 6 oz.) body only, including battery.
With the 50mm f/1.8 lens: 820g (28-15/16 ozs.).
With the 50mm f/1.4 lens: 925g (32-5/8 ozs.).

Motor Drive MA Unit ...Usable for: A-1
Structure: Grip type, composed of a motor for film winding, an electromagnetic clutch, a set of gears and a shutter release button.
Dimensions and Weight: 151mm (W) × 67mm (D) × 80mm (H) (5-15/16" × 2-5/8" × 3-1/8"), 200g (7 ozs.).

Ni-Cd Pack MA ...Usable for: A-1

Structure: Consists of a motor control circuit with an automatic stop circuit, Ni-Cd battery, a vertical position shutter release button and a selector switch. **Shooting Modes:** Three changeable modes: H (4 frames/sec.) L (3 frames/sec.) and S (single frames). **Battery Life:** (H mode with 36 exposure film) Normal Temperatures: 60 rolls or more. Low Temperatures: (−10°C): 15 rolls or more. **Operable Temperature Range:** −20°C ~ +40°C. **Power Source:** Built-in Ni-Cd batteries, 14.4V. Rechargeable. **Dimensions and Weight:** 151mm (W) × 61mm (D) × 29mm (H) (5-15/16″ × 2-3/8″ × 1-1/8″), 205g (7 ozs.).

Battery Pack MA ...Usable for A-1

Structure: Consists of a motor control circuit with an automatic stop circuit, a battery magazine for penlight (size AA) batteries, a vertical position shutter release button, an instant high speed mode button and a selector switch. **Shooting Modes:** Three changeable modes: H (5 frames/sec.), L (3.5 frames/sec.) and S (single frames). **Battery Life:** (H mode with 36-exposure film) Normal Temperatures: 60 rolls or more. Low Temperatures: (−10°C): 5 rolls or more. **Operable Temperature Range:** −10°C ~ +45°C. **Power Source:** 18 volts (12 penlight size AA batteries). **Dimensions and Weight:** 151mm (W) × 67mm (D) × 40mm (H) (5-15/16″ × 2 5/8″ × 1-9/16″), 395g (13 ozs.) including batteries.

Wireless Controller LC-1 ...Usable for: A-1

Transmitter

Power Source: Two penlight alkaline manganese batteries. **Recycling Time:** One second or less. **Number of Channels:** Three. Indications for CH1, CH2, and CH3. **Light Wavelength:** Approx. 700nm or more. **Size and Weight:** 49mm (W) × 120mm (D) × 37mm (H) (1-15/16″ × 4-3/4″ × 1-1/2″), 172g (6 ozs.) including batteries.

Receiver ...Usable for: A-1

Power Source: One 006P battery (DC 9V). **Recycling Time:** 0.5 sec. or less. **Wavelength of Receiving Light:** Approx. 900nm (peak value). **Number of Channels:** Three. CH1, CH2, CH3. **Switch:** S, C. Sliding type. (S: single. C: continuous). **Attachment:** Onto the camera's accessory shoe. **Size and Weight:** 35mm (W) × 62mm (D) × 84.5mm (H) (1-3/8″ × 2-7/16″ × 3-5/16″), 153g (5 ozs.) including batteries.

CANON AT-1

Type: 35mm SLR (Single-Lens-Reflex) camera with focal plane shutter.
Usable Lenses: Canon FD series with full aperture metering, Canon FL series with stopped-down metering.
Field of View: 93.5% vertical and 96.3% horizontal coverage of the actual picture area.
Viewfinder Information: Split-image/microprism rangefinder, circular aperture needle with meter needle and proper metering zone index marks, the upper one of which doubles as battery power level check mark.
Exposure Meter: Built-in. Using CdS photocell. Coupled to shutter speeds, film speeds, and f/stops. Match needle type, TTL full aperture metering mechanism.
Exposure Meter Coupling Range: With ASA 100 film, EV3 (f/1.4, 1/4 of a second) to EV17 (f/16, 1/500 of a second) at ASA 100 film with FD 50mm f/1.4 lens.
Film Speed Range: ASA 25 to ASA 3200.
Shutter Speeds: 1/1000 ~ 1, 2, B.
Self-Timer: Electronically controlled self-timer. It releases the shutter after a lag of 10 seconds. A red LED lamp revealed blinks on and off to indicate its operation.
Power Source: One 6.2V silver oxide battery only (UCAR Eveready No. 544, Mallory PX28). The battery lasts approximately one year under normal use.
Flash Synchronization: X synchronization is at 1/60 second. M synchronization is at 1/30 second and below.
Automatic Flash: With the Canon Speedlite 133A, 155A, 177A and 199A, the shutter speed is automatically set at 1/60 of a second except when the shutter dial is set at "B" though the prescribed aperture should be set manually. The amount of light is automatically controlled for correct flash exposure.
Back Cover: Opened by pulling up rewind knob. Removable for attaching Data Back A. With memo holder.
Film Advance Lever: Single stroke with 120° throw and stand-off angle of 30°. Film can be wound with several short strokes. The Canon Power Winder A winds film automatically.
Frame Counter: Additive type, automatically resets itself when the back cover is opened. While rewinding film, it counts the frame numbers downward.
Size: 141 × 87 × 47.5mm (5-9/16″ × 3-7/16″ × 1-7/8″) (body only)
Weight: 590g (20-13/16 ozs.) (body only)
790g (27-7/8 ozs.) with the 50mm f/1.8 lens.

Subject to change without notice.

1800
The modern Camera Obscura, a portable reflex camera

1839 The Giroux Daguerrotype Camera by Alphonse Giroux

1841
Voigtlander's all metal camera (with f/3.4 lens)

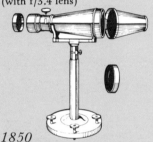

1850
Scott Archer's Wet Collodion Process

1853 The Scott Archer Wet Collodion Process Camera

1870
Silver bromide gelatin emulsion developed by R. Maddox

1884
Development of Monocular Duflex The Shoe Reflector (with mirror shutter)
- Lens interchangeability
- No parallax problem
- Able to focus through the view-finder
- A big step in development of focal plane shutter

1888
Invention of roll film and Anschutz focal plane shutter

1888
Introduction of The Kodak with 100 sheets of paper negatives (camera and film sent to camera manufacturer for development)

1888
The Thornton Pickard field camera

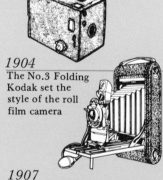

1900 Introduction of No.1 Brownie camera by Eastman Kodak

1901
Introduction of No.2 Brownie

1904
The No.3 Folding Kodak set the style of the roll film camera

1907
The 3A Autograflex, forerunner of the cellulose film type SLR

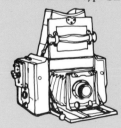

1910
The Tourist Multiple, world's first 35mm camera (half-frame, 750 exposures)

1912
The Vest Pocket Kodak

1913
The Ika Atom 51 (considered to be the prototype of the spring camera)

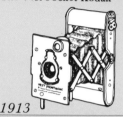

1915 The Speedgraphic

1915
The Minigraph (half-frame, 50 exposures)

1924
The Ermanox

1925
The Ansco Memo (half-frame, 50 exposures)

1925
The Leica 1A by Oscar Barnack and Ernst Leitz (the first modern 35mm camera)

1929
Enter the film camera age with the Rolleiflex by Franke and Heidecke

1932
The Contax I by Zeiss Ikon

1933 The Hansa Canon

1933 The Plaubel Makina

1934 The Exakta 127A Ihagee

1935
The Zeiss Ikon Contaflex (a 35mm twin-lens reflex)

1936
The Kine Exakta Ihagee (beginnings of the 35mm SLR)

1938
The Super Kodak 620 (the first automatic exposure camera)

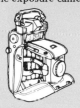

1941
Kodak Ektra

1941
The Kodak Medalist (a 6 x 9 format rangefinder camera)

1942
The Mercury Univex

1943
Introduction of the Kardon from Premier Instruments Corp.

1948
The Hasselblad 6 x 6 SLR

1950
The first Pentaprism-type SLR, the Contax S VEB

1954
The Asahiflex II (realization of the quick-return mirror)

1954
The Leica M3 by Ernst Leitz

1959
The Nikon F (a long-run pro SLR)

1961 The Canon Canonet

1963 The Kodak Motormatic

1963
The Kodak Instamatic

1963
The Olympus Pen F (a half-frame SLR)

1965
The Pellix from Canon (with Pellicle mirror)

1966
The Polaroid Automatic 100 Land Camera with electronic shutter and automatic exposure (introduction of Polacolor)

1970
The Polaroid SX-70 (color pictures appear before your very eyes)

1970
The Canondate E (realization of automatic data imprinting)

1970
The Rollei 35 (a compact 35mm)

1972
The Kodak 110 Pocket Camera

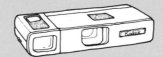

1971
The Canon F-1

1975 The Contax RTS

1976
The Canon AE-1 (first electronic shutter-speed priority automatic SLR)

1976 The Kodak Instant EK-6

1977
The Canon A-1 (a multi-mode automatic SLR)

1978
The Polaroid Sonar Autofocus

1979 The Kodak Electromax

1979
The Canon AF35M (an automatic focus 35mm)

The world's first photograph, a "heliograph", 100
by Joseph Nicéphore Niépce, 1826.

A Daguerrotype, 101
c.1840.

An 1840 Calotype, The Ruins of Pompeii, by 102
Calvert Jones, an associate of William Henry Fox
Talbot.

The camera obscura method of producing indoors an image of the outside scenery was discovered several centuries before the photograph. It was in the 11th century that the Arabs were experimenting with opening a hole in one side of the tent and viewing the image on the other. This discovery didn't reach Europe until the 15th century and wasn't really applied until the end of the 17th. The form it took was that of a movable room or sedan chair. Artists would put a piece of translucent paper over the ground-glass viewing screen and then trace the image, thus giving perspective.

Then, in 1686, a German monk by the name of Johann Zahn came up with the first portable model of a camera obscura. A wooden box a mere nine inches high and two feet long, it had a single lens inside a tube that could be moved for focus control, a diaphragm to control the light and a mirror to reflect the image onto a translucent viewing screen. This camera was the forerunner of the modern SLR. It was, of course, a great improvement but there was still one thing wrong. Preserving the image literally required the skill of an artist. Here is where a man named Joseph Nicéphore Niépce entered the scene in 1826.

This French lithographer and inventor knew that asphalt hardens when struck by sunlight. He mixed up a solution of asphalt and lavender oil and coated a sheet of pewter with the concoction. The pewter was then inserted into a camera obscura which was left on a windowsill. An incredible exposure time of eight hours was required, but by this method, Niépce produced the world's first photograph which he called a heliograph.

Already, 40% of the foundation of modern photographic technology was laid. Developments followed one after another with perhaps the most important, developing, being introduced in 1839 by Niépce's assistant, one Louis Jacques Mandé Daguèrre. His Daguerrotype was a silver-plated copper sheet sensitized by vapor from iodine crystals. After an exposure of 30 minutes and "developing" with some mercury vapor, an unbelievably (for those times) sharp picture resulted.

Almost simultaneous with the Daguerrotype, however, an English inventor named William Henry Fox Talbot was experimenting with salt. Applying this substance to sheets of paper and thus light-sensitizing them, he would make silhouettes, in other words, a negative. This "negative" was then placed on a second piece of sensitized paper and sandwiched in between glass. A "positive" image could then be produced by letting sunlight strike this glass. From there, Talbot developed a special negative paper that recorded the image which would not appear until special chemicals were applied. He called this process the Calotype, from two Greek words meaning "beautiful" and "impression". The Calotype was a much easier system than the Daguerrotype but because of the paper fibers, its sharpness never attained the perfection of the latter.

To eradicate this problem, a cousin of Niépce, Abel Niépce de St. Victor, got the idea of using glass plates and a silver emulsion suspended in egg white. But soon, a substance named collodion was developed and in 1850 applied to photography by Robert Bingham of Great Britain. Made from cellulose nitrate, it took the place of the egg white and reduced the exposure time to about 5 seconds. Although the images obtained with these materials were relatively sharp, mixing the egg white or collodion and manipulating the heavy glass proved to be rather impractical. Also, the picture would have to be taken and developed while the solution was still wet; sensitivity loss occurred as the solution dried. That is why this process was known as "wet-plate photography". Nevertheless, this form of photography was popular and used with great success by such people as William Henry Jackson and Roger Fenton.

103

The Chess Players,
a William Henry Fox Talbot
Calotype, 1842.

Field Kitchen of the 8th Hussars, the Crimea. 104
A Roger Fenton wet plate, 1855.

Encampment of Horse Artillery, the Crimea, 105
a wet plate by Roger Fenton, 1855.

Children with Water Bottles, photographer unknown. Taken with Kodak American Film, C. 1890. 106

Around the same time that the wet collodion process was developed, a special lens designed by a University of Vienna professor, Josef Max Petzval, and camera built by Viennese instrument maker Peter von Voigtländer were introduced. The lens used on this camera was 16 times faster than that used by Daguerre and became, for 60 years, the photographer's standard lens.

An 1885 dry plate, Motion Study of a Girl Playing with a 107
Handkerchief, by Eadweard Muybridge.

The labor of the photographer handling wet plates was due to end and, in 1871, an English doctor by the name of Richard L. Maddox invented the first fast-drying emulsion made of gelatin. This quick-dry plate enabled a film sensitivity 60 times that of the wet plates. Along with that, exposure time was shortened and freezing a subject's movement finally became possible. Before it could become reality, however, a certain addition to the camera had to be made: the shutter. In 1861, the first focal plane shutter that allowed up to 1/500 sec. speeds was introduced and in 1887 the leaf shutter was invented by Edward Bausch. In the 1880's, a wide variety of cameras, some quite unusual, came on the market. There were giant cameras, multi-lens cameras that put many images on one sensitized plate, stereo cameras for 3-D-like pictures, panorama cameras and so on. However, they all had one fault —pictures had to be taken one at a time by inserting a sensitized plate, exposing it, taking it out and putting in another one. The high cost of this process was also not to an amateur's liking.

His knight-in-shining-armor appeared in 1888, in the form of George Eastman and his Kodak No.1. Several years prior to this, Eastman had come up with a silver bromide/gelatin coating for film that enabled it to be mass-produced on paper. It became known as "American Film".The Kodak camera came equipped with 100-exposure film. Since the opaque emulsion had to be peeled off the paper, a time-consuming process requiring a bit of dexterity, the camera with film still inside was sent to Eastman's factory for development of the exposed film and reloading of the camera. In spite of this drawback, the Kodak was epoch-making. It was the first to use roll film and the first that could be hand-carried, perfect for the amateur.

From that time on, improvements in camera design came fast and furious. In 1925, for example, there was the compact Leica that could take almost any kind of picture under any condition. It came equipped with a fast focal plane shutter, high-performance f/3.5 lens making indoor photography possible, a viewfinder with built-in rangefinder, and it could accept 36-exposure 35mm film. Further refinements such as one knob to advance the film and simultaneously cock the shutter, even faster lenses and the twin-lens reflex with two lenses —one for picture-taking and one for focusing— appeared during the latter part of the 1920's and early 1930's.

Then, in 1936, a small camera was introduced that allowed easy focusing through the taking lens. Known as the Kine Exakta, this advancement enabled images to be captured just as they were seen in the viewfinder. The age of the 35mm SLR had arrived.

Cameras could not have progressed without one more improvement in film. Almost simultaneous with the introduction of the Kodak, Hannibal Goodwin, a New Jersey clergyman, filed a patent application for a different kind of roll film based on flexible celluloid. Although the Eastman Company also came out with a version of the film, resulting in a drawn-out legal battle, this is neither here nor there. This breakthrough was responsible for the design revolution that has given us the modern SLR. Perhaps in the future, other film changes will occur, just like the recent introduction of ASA 400 color film, that will shift the whole course of photography. It promises to be an interesting time.

Your camera is a marvelous precision instrument. It is indeed rugged in the sense that it will give you hundreds of thousands of memorable pictures as long as you treat it with respect.

Nemeses

If a camera had enemies, they would certainly be moisture, including excessive humidity, dust, sand, salt, excessive heat and the use of force. If your camera should get just a little wet from drops of rain or melted snow, wipe it off right away with a clean, dry, soft cloth. If you intend to shoot pictures in the rain, you should take every precaution to keep the camera and lens dry. Fashion a protective covering from a plastic bag and have someone hold an umbrella over you. If you should be so unfortunate as to actually drop your camera in water, do rush it to the nearest Canon service facility to see if anything can be done. Even so, chances are the only thing the service people will be able to do is to perform a post-mortem.

If you live or travel in an area which is excessively humid during certain seasons, special care must be taken in storing the camera and lens. That is, take care to store them in as dry an area as possible, with a desiccant such as silica gel. Clean your lenses often and regularly, as it is otherwise possible for harmful mildew to form on the glass surfaces.

Excessive heat is as bad for the film as it is for the camera. Just to list a few places NOT to put your camera, there are the rear shelf and glove compartment of your car, on a radiator, in front of a heat register or sitting in direct sunlight. As a precaution against the possibility of the film getting fogged or the shutter burned, it is advisable not to set the camera lens-up with the lens uncapped in direct sunlight. The lens should always be capped unless you are shooting anyway.

With water, sand, salt and excessive heat being among your camera's worst enemies, it is not hard to guess what place it hates the most —the beach. It is most important to keep your equipment well protected in a case in the shade. Never but never store it in a dark-colored bag in the sun, and take care not to let any sand seep in. Sand is just plain destructive. It can be troublesome enough if it gets lodged in crevices on the camera's or lens' exterior, but you should, at all costs, avoid letting it into the interior. If it is a windy day and there is the slightest chance that sand may enter, it is best not to change the film or the lens. Even if no drastic accident occurs, the camera will probably be exposed to moisture and salt in the air. All of your equipment will need a thorough cleaning as soon as possible after you get off the beach.

Giving the Camera a Professional Cleaning Job

If you clean your camera as follows, you will never have to ask a professional to do it. The materials you will need for this as well as for cleaning the lens can all be found in your local camera store. To clean the camera, a soft (camel)-haired brush (lens brush or blower brush usually) and a silicone cloth or a chamois are necessary.

With the lens still attached to prevent dust from entering inside the camera, first blow-brush dust off the camera's exterior.

Do this especially well after exposing it to sand, and pay particular attention to areas around the shutter button and the film advance lever. Then polish the camera with the silicone cloth or the chamois. Do not use these cloths on the eyepiece, which should be cleaned in the same way as the lens.

If the camera has been used on the beach and you think some salt may still be on the body, you may wish to wipe the external metal areas with a clean, soft cloth which has been moistened slightly with metal cleaning fluid.

Then open the camera back and carefully blow-brush the film chamber, take-up spool, sprocket and film rails. Film dust, which may scratch a new roll of film, tends to collect in these areas. Be very careful not to touch or put pressure on the sensitive shutter curtain and pressure plate.

If the mirror gets dirty, remember that it will only affect the clarity of the image you see in the viewfinder; the picture will be just fine. The mirror is an extremely delicate part of the camera which should be cleaned only when absolutely necessary. All you should do is blow off dust very gently with a blower brush, not even using the brush part. If it really needs further cleaning, please send the camera to your nearest Canon service facility and let the professionals do it this time.

Precaution

There are cans of pressurized air on the market which are made for blowing dust out of corners on the exterior of the camera and lens. They should never be used on the mirror or shutter curtain which could end up "blowing" along with the dust. If you use one of these products make sure to follow its instructions, especially those concerning how to hold it—upright.

Now for the Lens and Other Glass Surfaces

One big favor you can do for your lenses, as was mentioned earlier, is to keep each equipped with a UV or Skylight filter at all times and with the front cap on when you are not shooting. The filter is an inexpensive, easily replaceable accessory which will protect the lens surface from dirt and scratches.

Dirt and smudges on a lens cause flare which scatters light rays and results in dull, low-contrast pictures. Also, if dirt is left on a lens for a long time, it may leave spots even after cleaning, so it is best to clean your lenses regularly.

To clean the exterior of the lens, you may use the same blower brush and silicone cloth (or lens brush and chamois) you used for the camera and in the same way: brush first, then polish with the cloth.

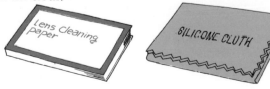

For cleaning the glass surfaces of the lens and the camera's eyepiece you will need another camel-hair brush or one of equivalent softness —a second lens brush or blower brush is perfect. Don't use the same one you use for the external parts of the camera and lens. It may pick up dirt which will scratch the glass. For wiping off smudges, lens-cleaning fluid and lens tissue are necessary. Rubbing alcohol (pure ethyl or methyl alcohol), which is handy for its quick-drying properties, may be substituted for the lens-cleaning fluid. Make sure the lens tissue is the kind made for cleaning camera lenses and not eyeglasses. Facial tissue and any other kind of tissue which may be impregnated with a chemical are also out. Usually they are either too harsh or the chemical will ruin the lens' coating, which is so carefully and expensively applied in the factory to reduce ghost and flare and assure good color reproduction. For the same reasons, never use a silicone cloth on the glass surfaces. A very clean, soft, lint-free cloth may be used, but lens tissue is generally easier and better. The cotton swab-tipped sticks, which are commercially available, are very handy for getting into the corners of the eyepiece after blow-brushing.

Tip the lens downwards and blow-brush off the dust and dirt. Inspect the surface at an angle to see that all dust has been removed. Now fold the lens tissue into a triangle and squeeze one or two drops of lens-cleaning fluid or pure alcohol on it. Don't soak it and never squeeze liquid directly on the lens surface. Some could seep in at the edges inside the lens barrel where it will cause untold havoc. Starting at the center, wipe the lens in a circular, unidirectional motion, slowly working towards the edges. Do this two or three times with new pieces of lens tissue or different corners of the cloth you are using.

Now it's time to inspect your handiwork. Breathe on the lens to cloud it up. If the cloud evaporates in a slowly constricting circle, the lens is clean. If the circle loses its shape, that part of the lens is still dirty. All filters, close-up lenses, extenders and other lens attachments should be kept clean in this same manner.

Parts Check

From time to time it is a good precaution to check that all of the camera's parts are in working order. It's much better to catch a problem while you are cleaning your equipment than at the very moment you want to take some important pictures. Operate the film advance and rewind levers and the self-timer. Check the frame counter and the battery. With the camera back open, trip the shutter to see that it travels as it should. Trip the shutter again while looking through the front of the lens to see that the diaphragm is closing down perfectly. Try it at every aperture. Even keeping an eye on the condition of your neckstrap is important. Replace it if it is worn. If you have a commercially-available one that attaches to the camera by metal clasps, make sure the clasps are closed. You would be surprised at the strange things that can happen.

If ever you come across some part that isn't working, please remember that forcing it will only exacerbate the problem. Take the camera to a Canon service center for professional attention.

Storage

If you use your camera frequently and handle it with care, you are doing the best possible thing for it. You can store your equipment for short periods of time in their individual cases.

If you must store the camera for several weeks to months, it is most important to keep in mind the camera's enemies. Store it in a cool, dry, dust-free area. Remove the battery first, so that it has no chance of leaking and corroding the camera's electrical contacts. Cap the lens, and if you store it separately from the camera, attach its rear cap and the camera's body cap.

Your equipment will not like being cooped up in a dark, dank case or bag any more than you would. Remove all of your equipment from the camera bag and from individual cases. Don't store them with moth balls or near corrosive chemicals in a laboratory. If you have one, a steel or glass-doored cabinet is a good place to store everything.

Sending Equipment for Repair

In the event that a piece of your equipment must be shipped to a Canon Factory Service Center or Authorized Service Facility, it must be packed to withstand the hazards of transport. The original packing material and box are the ideal packaging, even at that, it needs a little more surrounding material for going through normal mail. If you didn't save it, place the equipment in a container or carton which is large enough to leave plenty of space for padding. If you don't have any material made specially for packing, use newspaper for padding. It's always a good precaution to enclose your name and address on the inside. Make sure that the equipment is packed tight, showing no signs of movement after it is sealed. Label the package with your name and address —legibly, of course— and insure your equipment with your shipper.

Q&A

In spite of the many instruction booklets and brochures put out by Canon, a lot of people find they still have questions concerning their equipment. This section will try to clear up some of the most often asked ones.

Q.1 What kind of battery should I use?

A. Use either a 6V silver oxide or alkaline manganese battery. However, for the AT-1, use a silver oxide battery only. On the basis of extensive tests, the following brands of batteries are recommended.
Silver Oxide: UCAR—Eveready No.544, Mallory—PX28
Alkaline Manganese: UCAR—Eveready No.537

Q.2 What will happen when the battery starts to lose power?

A. As the battery starts to lose power, this fact will be so indicated in your camera's viewfinder. If it is indicated that battery power is below standard, the battery should be replaced with a new one. Even if you should fail to realize this, there is no problem. A safety device on the camera will activate and essentially lock the shutter button, preventing you from taking a picture. Without this safety device, your picture would come out wrongly exposed. Anyway, as long as the shutter is working, the camera can be safely used. (The battery check method will differ depending on the camera. Refer to Part Three, from page 52.)

Q.3 The camera comes with a case. Is it better to use the camera with the case on?

A. Hanging from your shoulder or neck, your camera will often bump against things and get dented or scratched. It must therefore be protected with the case. For power winder-driven pictures and in places where there are no objects to bump into, it will be more convenient to use the camera without the case as it will get in the way. The cam-

era also fits better in your hands without the case. Professional photographers usually use the camera without a case because, apart from the above, it is troublesome to take the case off each time film is changed, especially when taking many pictures.

Q.4 What can I do when the eyepiece or lens get fogged up?

A. Fogging occurs due to differences in temperature. If the camera and lens are very cold, they can be wiped with a clean, soft cloth, though they will soon get fogged up again. The best way to solve this problem is to let your equipment get warm and clear up naturally. However, do not do this under direct sunlight or near a heat source. Select a place in the shade where there is good ventilation.

Q.5 How should I go about selecting a dioptric lens for my A series camera?

A. For all A series cameras, if it is possible to see an object clearly at one meter (3.3 ft.), either with the naked eye or with eyeglasses, then it will be possible to see it clearly in the viewfinder. For those who cannot see the object clearly one meter away or who don't like to wear glasses when photographing, dioptric lenses are necessary. If you are such a person, contact your nearest camera dealer and see if they have a full line, or go to your nearest Canon facility. It is essential that you try various types to get the one that is best. You cannot take in your glasses prescription and expect the same dioptric lens as classifications are different. As a general rule, "—" is for nearsightedness and "+" is for farsightedness.

Q.6 What would happen if I were accidentally to take a picture with the FD lens' aperture ring off the "A" mark?

A. If the aperture ring is off "A", the automatic exposure mechanism will not work and the proper exposure will not be obtained (AE-1, AE-1 PROGRAM and A-1 only).
The picture will be taken at the aperture value that the aperture ring is turned to, which probably will not give proper exposure. If you do get correct exposure, consider it to be a fluke.

Q.7 I have an AV-1. What would be the results if I were to take a picture with the aperture ring on "A"?

A. The minimum aperture of the lens will become the aperture value with the shutter speed automatically selected accordingly. However, this shutter speed will often be slow, giving rise to camera movement problems.

Q.8 Can focusing screens be interchanged?

A. This cannot be done with the AE-1, AV-1 or AT-1. However, it is possible with the A-1 and AE-1 PROGRAM.
With the A-1 you have a choice of 7 types and with the AE-1 PROGRAM 8 different screens. With the AE-1 PROGRAM you can change them yourself using the special tool provided, but it is inadvisable with the A-1. Have it done at a Canon service station.

Q.9 Is the camera made of plastic?

A. Not all of the camera, only a part of it. Space-age plastic is used for the top cover (i.e., the exterior excluding the bottom plate). This makes the camera lighter than would be the case if metal was used and also helps prevent electric shocks. Replacing metal with plastic also eliminates the old problem of moisture forming on metal parts due to temperature change.

The body skeleton of the AE-1, AE-1 PROGRAM, A-1 and AT-1 is made totally of aluminum diecast, while plastic is used for a part of the AV-1's body skeleton.

Q.10 How can I lock exposure?
A. The AE-1 PROGRAM has an AE Lock Switch. There is no exposure lock provision on the AE-1 and AV-1. You could, however, try the following method with the AE-1. Take an exposure reading of the desired subject, find the aperture value indicated in the viewfinder and, removing the aperture ring from "A", set it on the indicated value. This is actually what is known as manual exposure.

Q.11 Is there some way to prevent ghost images?
A. A lens hood should be used, but for taking pictures directly towards bright light sources, the camera should be pointed at a slight angle, rather than straight on.

Q.12 Is there an adapter for using a lens of a different make on a Canon A series camera?
A. No. Ask the lens company whether they have an FD Canon mount for their lenses.

Q.13 Will the automatic advantages of my A series camera be kept intact if I use a different company's lenses?
A. Ask the company which made the lens whether they have an FD mount that will enable your camera to be used on automatic.

Q.14 What would be the results if a non-Canon lens were used on my A series camera?
A. Although there would probably be no problem, this isn't recommended for two big reasons. One is that Canon's lenses are made especially for its cameras. All pins and levers on the lens align perfectly with parts on the camera, ensuring exact signal transmission. You are taking a chance by using other makes of lenses that alignment may not be perfect. Also, Canon has put very high quality materials into its lenses to give you the sharpest image possible.

Q.15 Can Canon FL lenses be used on all A series cameras?
A. Four FL lenses cannot be mounted: FL 19mm f/3.5, FL 35mm f/2.5, FL 50mm f/1.8 and FL 58mm f/1.2. Any other FL lenses can be used. See your instruction booklet for further details.

Q.16 Can Ni-Cd batteries be used for the Power Winder A and Speedlites?
A. Ni-Cd batteries can be used for all of Canon's A series dedicated Speedlites but cannot be used for the Power Winder A. The reason for this is that the electrical current is higher than that of carbon-zinc and alkaline batteries which gives too strong a pull at the end of the film. This causes some film to tear.

Q.17 Is there a camera case which can house an A series camera with the Data Back A attached?
A. No. The design of this accessory requires that such a case be open in the back to allow manipulation of the dials. Not too practical.

Q.18 Can the Motor Drive MA be used on the AE-1?
A. No. But it can be used on the AE-1 PROGRAM and A-1.

Q.19 Can I use a flash unit other than a Canon Speedlite on my A series camera?
A. A dedicated flash from another company cannot be used on the hot shoe as its contact points will probably be different, which could burn out the camera's circuitry. This kind of flash should be placed on a separate flash bracket, with its synchro cord (if there is one) inserted into the camera's PC socket. A non-dedicated flash may be used on the camera's hot shoe, though it should be turned off while mounting. (The AV-1 has no PC socket, so a Canon Hot Shoe Adapter has to be attached to the hot shoe and the cord inserted into the adapter socket. This adapter can also be used in place of the flash bracket for dedicated flashes.)

For exposure, set the aperture to the value indicated by your flash's calculator dial. If it doesn't have one, you can calculate by dividing the flash's guide number by the shooting distance.

Q.20 There are old all-chrome and new all-black FD lenses. What is the difference between the two and why do some of the older lenses have SSC written on the lens while the new ones do not?
A. Both have the same breech-lock mount and signal transmission system. The old lenses are mounted on the camera by turning the tightening ring but with the new ones, the whole lens is turned to move a part hidden in the interior, corresponding to the tightening ring. This makes the new lenses slightly easier and quicker to mount and dismount. SSC stands for Super Spectra Coating, Canon's multi-layer coating which is now applied to almost every new FD lens. That is why it is no longer written on the lens itself.

Q.21 Does dust in the viewfinder have any effect on my pictures?
A. No, unless the dust is on the lens. Usually, this viewfinder dust is actually on the mirror, on the underside of the screen, inside the top cover or behind the eyepiece. It can be cleaned at a Canon service facility. If you decide to do it yourself, use only air for any internal viewing devices.

Q.22 What should I do if half of the split-image rangefinder darkens in dim light or with a lens having a maximum aperture of f/4 or smaller?
A. This is a natural phenomenon so there is no need to worry. If it happens, you should use the surrounding microprism or matte areas for focusing or try moving your eye slightly to the left or right. There is a usually a position at which it will clear.

Canon's World Wide Warranty that comes with your equipment is your protection against any breakdowns that may infrequently occur. As you can see from the list on these two pages, the service network is indeed world-wide. Just in America, there are eight major service stations you have to choose from plus numerous camera shops that have been specially authorized to handle Canon equipment. If you take your equipment in to them, you can be sure that it will be in good hands because these shops are guaranteed and in many cases, specially trained, by the N.Y. head office.

The same reliability is true the world over as well. If anything should happen while you're travelling, repairs will be done with the professionalism which has become Canon's trademark.

CANON FACTORY SERVICE CENTERS IN U.S.A. AND CANADA

CANON U.S.A., INC. NEW YORK OFFICE	One Canon Plaza, Lake Success, Long Island, N.Y. 11042 Tel. (516) 488-6700
MANHATTAN SS	600 Third Avenue, New York, N.Y. 10016 Tel. (212) 557-2400
CHICAGO OFFICE	140 Industrial Drive, Elmhurst, Illinois 60126 Tel. (312) 833-3070
COSTA MESA OFFICE	123 Paularino Avenue East, Costa Mesa, California 92626 Tel. (714) 979-6000
LOS ANGELES OFFICE	3321 Wilshire Blvd., Los Angeles, California 90010 Tel. (213) 387-5010
SAN FRANCISCO SS	776 Market Street, San Francisco, California 94102 Tel. (415) 433-5640
ATLANTA OFFICE	6380 Peachtree Industrial Blvd., Norcross, Georgia 30071 Tel. (404) 448-1430
HAWAII OFFICE	Bldg. B-2, 1050 Ala Moana Blvd., Honolulu, Hawaii 96814 Tel. (808) 521-0361

CANON OPTICS & BUSINESS MACHINES CANADA, LTD.

TORONTO OFFICE	3245 American Drive Mississauga, Ontario L4V 1N4 Tel. 416-678-2730
MONTREAL SERVICE CENTRE	6969 Route Transcanadienne Bureau 117 St. Laurent PQ H4T 1V8 Tel. 514-332-3514
VANCOUVER OFFICE	5900A No. 2 Road, Richmond, BC V7C 4R9 Tel. 604-278-3311
EDMONTON SS	5222-86 St. Edmonton, Alberta T6E 5J6 Tel. 403-468-1818

CANON U.S.A. INC. AUTHORIZED SERVICE FACILITIES

U.S.A.

ALABAMA Bush and Millimaki
902 Bob Wallace Avenue, S.E. Huntsville, Alabama 35801
ALASKA Dan's Camera Repair
Between G & H Streets, 735 West 4th Avenue, Anchorage, Alaska
ARIZONA Phoenix Camera Repair, Inc.
3232 North 16th Street, Phoenix, Arizona 85016
CALIFORNIA AV Repair Corp.
1411 El Camino Real, Mountain View, California 94040
Camera Repair Service
380 14th Street, Oakland, California 94612
Central Camera Repair
605 "C" Street, San Diego, California 92101
R.M. Cudabac Camera Repair
184 2nd Street, San Francisco, California 94105
Gerhard's Camera Repair Service
137 S. Vermont Avenue, Los Angeles, California 90004
Graf's Camera Repair, Inc.
4129 Beverly Blvd., Los Angeles, California 90004
Jimmies Camera Repair
7129 Balboa Blvd., Van Nuys, California 91406
Kurt's Camera Repair
7805 Mission Gorge Road, San Diego, California 92120
Little Tokyo Camera
312 E. 1st Street, Los Angeles, California 90012
Professional Photo Repair
1725 "L" Street, Sacramento, California 95814
Universal Precision Inst. Co.
1570 4th Street, San Rafael, California 92701
COLORADO Metro Camera Svce., Inc.
1965 S. Federal Blvd., Denver, Colorado 80219
Rocky Mountain Camera Repair
240 Broadway, Denver, Colorado 80203
DISTRICT OF COLUMBIA SPTS Washington, DC, Inc.
1240 Mt. Olivet Road N.E., Washington, DC 20002
FLORIDA Photo Equipment Service
3222 S. Dixie, West Palm Beach, Florida 33405
SPTS, Jacksonville, Inc.
3241 Beach Blvd., Jacksonville, Florida 32207
SPTS, Miami, Inc.
14352 Biscayne Blvd., Miami, Florida 33181

SPTS, Orlando, Inc.
1201 North Mills Avenue, Orlando, Florida 32803
SPTS, St. Petersburg, Inc.
1750 Ninth Avenue North, St. Petersburg, Florida 33713
GEORGIA Camera Service Company
1270 Winchester Pkwy., S.E., Suite 129 Smyrna, Atlanta, Georgia 30080
Precision Camera Svc.
2005 North Ashley Street, Valdosta, Georgia 31601
HAWAII Photocine Servicenter, Inc.
765 Amana Street, Suite 204, Honolulu, Hawaii 96814
IDAHO Idaho Camera
806 Main Street, Boise, Idaho 83702
ILLINOIS International Camera Corp.
844 West Adama Street, Chicago, Illinois 60607
INDIANA Camera Repair Service
2070 East 54th Street, Suite 11, Indianapolis, Indiana 46220
KANSAS A & H Camera Repair, Inc.
915 N. Kansas, Topeka, Kansas 66608
KENTUCKY Camera Services, Inc.
216 S. Shelby Street, Louisville, Kentucky 40202
LOUISIANA SPTS, Inc.
3030-I-10 Service Road, Metairie, Louisiana 70001
MARYLAND Folkemer Photo Service
9041 Chevrolet Drive, Elicott City, Maryland 21043
MASSACHUSETTS Precision Camera Repair, Inc.
43 Sheridan Street, Chicopee Falls, Massachusetts 01020
Sanford's Photographic Inc.
1054 Massachusetts Avenue, Arlington, Massachusetts 02174
David Zuckerman Camera Repair Service
13 Rosewood Drive, Wordester, Massachusetts 01602
MICHIGAN Cahill Camera Service
7119 Puritan Avenue, Detroit, Michigan 48238
Midwest Camera Repairs, Inc.
328 Oak Street, Wyandotte, Michigan 48192
MINNESOTA Custom Camera Service
823 W. Lake Street, Minneapolis, Minnesota 55408
Marquette Camera Repair
903 Marquette Avenue, Minneapolis, Minnesota 55402
Northwest Camera Repair Co.
415 First Avenue North, Minneapolis, Minnesota 55401
MISSOURI Wasinger Kamera Klinic
110 S. Highway 67 Florissant, Missouri 63031
MONTANA Camera Crafts
4 North 29th Street, Billings, Montana 59101
NEBRASKA Lincoln Camera Repair, Inc.
611 North 27th Street, Lincoln, Nebraska 68503
NEW JERSEY Bergen Camera Repair Corp.
193 Route 17, Paramus, New Jersey 07653
Mack Camera Service
1025 Commerce Avenue, Union, New Jersey 07083
NEW YORK Photo Tech Repair Service Inc.
132 4th Avenue, New York, New York 10003
Continental Camera
1243 Abbott Road, Buffalo, New York 14218
Hudson Valley Camera & AV Repair Service, Inc.
199 West Route 59, Nanuet, New York 10954
Professional Camera Repair (SLR)
37 West 47th Street, New York, New York 10036
Russo Camera Repair Service
939 N. Salina Street, Syracuse, New York 13208
NORTH CAROLINA SPTS Charlotte, Inc.
2610 S. Blvd., Charlotte, North Carolina 28209
OHIO Camtronics
4345 North High Street, Columbus, Ohio 43214
Jim's Camera Repair
2060 Mason Street, Toledo, Ohio 43605
Precision Camera Repair Service
35 Tulip Road, Medway, Ohio 45341
OKLAHOMA Photo Products Repair
3109 Classen Blvd., Oklahoma City, Oklahoma 73118
OREGON Associated Camera Repair
3333 N.E. Sandy Blvd., Portland, Oregon 97232
Interstate Camera Service
2438 N.E. Sandy Blvd., Portland, Oregon 97211
PENNSYLVANIA Camera Repair Service
8 Smithfield Street, Pittsburgh, Pennsylvania 15222
Comet Camera Repair Shop, Inc.
1211 Arch Street, 4th Floor, Boyertown Building, Phildelphia Pennsylvania 19107
Optic Box
295 Beverly Road, Room 4, Pittsburgh, Pennsylvania 15216
PUERTO RICO General Camera Repair
4 Vieques Street, Hato Rey, Puerto Rico 00918
RHODE ISLAND United Camera, Inc.
297 Elmwood Avenue, Providence, Rhode Island 02907
TENNESSEE SPTS, Inc.
3388 Summer Avenue, Memphis, Tennessee 38122
TEXAS Archinal Photo Electro Service
3100 Commerce Street, Dallas, Texas 75246
Camera Services, Inc.
3407 South Shepherd, Houston, Texas 77098
Garland Camera & Repair Shop
304 Ridgewood Center, Garland, Texas 75040
Havel Camera Service
1504 Fredericksburg Road, San Antonio, Texas 78201
UTAH Forster's Camera Service
122 W. South Temple, Suite 101, Salt Lake City, Utah 84101
Inkley Photo Center
589 North Main Layton, Utah 84041
Jack David Camera Clinic
3-1/2 East 3rd, South Salt Lake City, Utah 84111
VIRGINIA Strauss Photo Technical Service
434 W. 21st Street, Norfolk, Virginia 23517
WASHINGTON Am-Pro Camera Repair
East 201 Sprague Avenue, Spokane, Washington 99202
Omega
839 106 N.E. Bellev Washington 90084
Photo-Tronics, Inc.
223 Westlake Avenue, North, Seattle, Washington 98109
WISCONSIN BDC Enterprises, Inc.
133 W. Johnson Street, Madison, Wisconsin 53703

CANADA

CANON O.B.M. CANADA LTD.
AUTHORIZED SERVICE FACILITIES

BRITISH COLUMBIA Artisan Instrument Service
113 Langley Street., Victoria, B.C.
HALIFAX Camera Repair Center
2623 Windsor Street, Halifax, Nova Scotia B3K 5C7
OTTAWA Camera Service Center
343 Somerset St. West, Ottawa, Ontario K2P OJ8
QUEBEC Camera Test & Service Inc. ENR
67 Boul. St.-Cyrille-Est, Suite 25, Quebec 4, P.Q. GIR 2A9
MANITOBA Eden Photo Ltd.
141 Sherbrook Street, Winnipeg, Manitoba

CANON FACTORY SERVICE CENTERS

AUSTRALIA MELBOURNE Canon Australia Pty. Ltd. Head Office
2 Hall Street, Hawthorn East Melbourne 3123
Phone: 03-20-1331
SYDNEY Canon Australia Pty. Ltd. Sydney Office
22 Lambs Road, Artarmon Sydney 2064
Phone: 439-3233
HONG KONG Canon Hongkong Trading Co., Ltd.
5th Fl., 2-6 Fui Yiu Kok St., Tsuen Wan, New Territories, P.O. Box 140
Phone: NT225261, 225262
REPUBLIC OF PANAMA Canon Latin America, Inc.
Apartado 2019, Colon Free Zone, Phone: 47-3476, 47-6820
THE NETHER-LANDS Canon Amsterdam nv (Camera Service Center)
Gebouw 70, Schiphol Oost, Phone: Amsterdam 173031

AFRICA

CANON AUTHORIZED SERVICE
FACILITIES AND SERVICE AGENCY

ANGOLA Rocha Monteiro
Rue Salvador Correira, 69-1 P.O. Box 2815 Luanda, Phone: 34395
CAMEROON C.C.H.A. Cameroon
P.O. Box 4030 Douala, Phone: 3590
EGYPT Rehabco Co.
10 Abi Emama Street, Dokki P.O. Box 1969, Cairo, Phone: 98 43 19
ISLE DE REUNION Maison Ah-Sing S.A.R.L.
59, Rue Alexis de Villeneuve B.P. 603 St. Denis, Phone: 212 780
MAURITIUS R. Canabady & Co. Ltd.
Dawood Building 1 Louis Pasteur Street B.P. 27 Port Louis, Phone: 2-2389
MOROCCO Cogedir
51 Rue Omar Slaoui, Casablanca, Phone: 76547
REPUBLIQUE DU SENEGAL Photo Cine Senegal
1, Place de l'Indépendance, P.O. Box 3266 Dakar, Phone: 224-73
SOMALIA Foto Stella
P.O. Box 697, Mogadishu, Phone: 3489
SOUTH AFRICA H. Platow Pty., Ltd.
P.O. Box 4456, Mayveen House, Corner, Nugget & President Streets, Johannesburg, Phone: 23-9006
SUDAN Cine & Photo Supply Co.
P.O. Box 393, Khartoum, Phone. 75162, 76943

ASIA

HONG KONG Jardine Marketing Services Ltd.
110 Prince's Building, Chater Road, Phone: 5-256031/4
MALAYSIA Guthrie SDN BHD. (Ghthrie Trading) Canon Division
33 Beach Street, P.O. Box 97, Penang, Phone: 2219161
SINGAPORE Guthrie Singapore Pte. Ltd. (Ghthrie Trading)
39, Sixth Avenue, Bukit Timah, P.O. Box 900 Singapore 10
Phone: 662555, 672555
THAILAND Fantarect Co., Ltd.
304-8, Mahaesak Road, Bangkok-5, Phone: 235-4040
TAIWAN Hung Chong Trading Co., Ltd.
20, Chiling Road, Taipei, Phone: 571-1166
PAKISTAN Kaderson Traders
Pakistan Museum Building, 1st Floor, Zaibunnisa Street, Saddar, Karachi-3
Phone: 51-43-08

CENTRAL & SOUTH AMERICA

ARGENTINA Direco, S.A.C.I.F.I.
Rivadavia 922-926, Piso 6, OF, 611, Buenos Aires, Phone: 38-4717, 38-0950
BERMUDA Stuarts' Distributing Company
P.O. Box 659, Hamilton, Phone: 2-0858
BRASIL Canon do Brasil Industria e Comercio Ltda.
Rua Domingos de Moraes 1576 Vila Mariana, Sao Paulo CEP-0410, S.P.
Phone: 544-1946
CHILE Lobenstein y Keller, S.A.
Casilla 12-D, Santiago, Phone: 87225, 69530
CURACAO Curacao Trading Co., (N.A.) N.V.
P.O. Box 308, Willemstad, Phone: 62-33724, 66-23217
MEXICO Canon Latinoamerica De Mexico, S.A.
AV. Cuauhtemoc 1230 Col. Santa Cruz Atoyac
Z.P. 13 Mexico D.F., Phone: 559-88-44, 559-86-19, 559-93-10
PERU Casa Hindu, S.A.
P.O. Box 4784, Lima, Phone: 286025
VENEZUELA Canon Venezolana S.A.
Edificio La Colonia Vennida Jalisco, Urbanización Las Mercedes, Caracas
Phone: 91-41-67

EUROPE

ANDORRA H. Cierco
Prada Ramon, Edificio Cierco, Andorre la Vieille, Phone: .078-21357
AUSTRIA Canon Gesellschaft m.b.H.
Modecenterstrasse 22 A-2, A-1030 Wien
Phone: 75-65-01
BELGIUM Geo Wehry & Cie S.A. Dept. Photo-Ciné
Grisarstraat 46, 1070 Brussels, Phone: 02/523.80.16
DENMARK Princo A.S.
7 Herstedvang, 2026 Albertslund, Phone: 646677

ENGLAND J.J. Silber Ltd.
Engineers Way, Wembley, Middlesex, HA9 OEA, Phone: 01-903-8081
FINLAND Oy Canon Ab
Hoylaamotie 14, SF 00380 Helsinki 38, Phone: 09/3580-55-88-61
FRANCE Canon France S.A.
30 Boulevard Vital-Bouhot, Ile de Jatte-92200, 92521 Neuilly sur Seine
Phone: 74791199
GREECE Le Cinéma
3 Stadium Street, 125 Athens, Phone: 3229020, 3236201
IRELAND Atlas Wholesale
5 Henry Place, Dublin 1, Phone: 745141/2/3
ITALY Canon Italia S.P.A.
Corso Milano 92/B, 37100 Verona, Phone: 045-56-2973
NORWAY Asec. A.S.
Stroemsveien 56 1473 Skarer, Phone: 707401
PORTUGAL Seque (Sociedade Nacional de Equipamentos, Lda)
Pr. Da Alegria, 58, 2° 1200 Lisboa, Phone: 320376/370082
SPAIN Focica S.A.
Avenida Diagonal 534 Barcelona 6
Phone: 200-1333/1565/1765
SWEDEN Canon Svenska AB
Stensätravägen 13, P.O. Box 2084, S-127 02 Skärholmen, Phone: 8-970420
SWITZERLAND Canon Optics S.A.
Max Hoggerstrasse 2,8048 Zurich, Phone: 643-424
THE NETHER-LANDS Borsumij Foto B.V. Dept. Canon Import
De Lasso 4, Roelofarendsveen, Phone: 01713-9013
WEST GERMANY Euro-Photo GmbH
4156 Willich 3-Schiefbahn, Linsellesstrasse 142-156
Phone: 02154-5095

MIDDLE EAST

BAHRAIN Green Flag Stores
Alkhalifa Road, Phone: 53246, 55224
CYPRUS Ntinos I., Kakoyiannis
25A Regaena Street, Flat No. 1, P.O. Box 1579, Nicosia, Phone: 64708
IRAN Aphomar
127, South Farah Ave. P.O. Box 486 Teheran
Phone: 852442/852444/855567
ISRAEL Karat Ltd.
Shalom Tower 10, Montefiori St., P.O. Box 29536, Tel-Aviv, Phone: 55244-5
REMETAM Industrial & Trading Co., Ltd.
128 Allenby Road, P.O. Box 262, Tel-Aviv, Phone: 622691, 622692
Eshkar Ltd.
9, Frishman Street, Tel-Aviv, Phone: 22 21 24
JORDAN Nizar A.R. Fayoumi
Amir Mohammad Street, P.O. Box 1014, Amman, Phone: 44605, 41661
KUWAIT Photo and Cine Equipment Co., Ltd.
Fahad Salem Street, P.O. Box 270, Phone: 422846 & 423801
LEBANON Eastern Photographic Co.
P.O. Box 3060, Beirut, Phone: 222757
PEOPLE'S DEMO-CRATIC REPUBLIC OF YEMEN The Popular Stores
The Crescent, Steamer Point, P.O. Box 1210, Aden
Phone: 22436
THE UNITED ARAB EMIRATES Jawad Yousuf Khoory & Bros.
P.O. Box 284, Dubai, Phone: 432168
SAUDI ARABIA Ali Zaid Al-Quraishi & Brothers
King Abdul Aziz Street, P.O. Box 1796, Jeddah, Phone: 31402, 30364
SYRIA Photo Garbis
P.O. Box 2040 Damascus, Phone: 44 84 47

OCEANIA

FIJI ISLANDS Pacific Mercantile Co., Ltd.
G.P.O. Box 240, Suva, Phone: 312722
NEW CALEDONIA Omnium Caledonien d'Importation
Rue de l'Espérance, Magenta, B.P. 2248, Noumea, Phone: 746-35
NEW ZEALAND Photographic Wholesalers Ltd.
246 Queen Street, P.O. Box 1159, Auckland-1, Phone: 364-660
PAPUA AND NEW GUINEA Oceania Indent Agency
P.O. Box 5518, Boroko, Port Moresby, Phone: PM 256406
TAHITI Maison Morgan Vernex
Rue Jeanne d'Arc B.P. 449 Papeete, Phone: 309

Contributing Photographers

Aoki, Koji. p.44(14), p.134(62)
CANON Medical Equipment Design Dept. p.21(6)
Digiacomo, Melchior p.123(44)
Furusawa, Shyoji. p.45(17)
Goto, Michio. p.151(82) (84)
Ikeba, Hiroshi. p.44(15), p.106-107(27), p.108(28)-(31) (32), p.125(48), p.131(56) (57),
          p.145(80), p.161(85), p.162(86)
Iooss, Walter Jr. p.135(64)
Kawashima, Akiyoshi. p.20(1), p.129(52)
Kihara, Kazuto. p.140(71)
Mase, Akira. p.79(21), p.123(47), p.135(63)
Matsumoto, Kiyokazu. p.63(20), p.155(91)
Miyazaki, Yoji. p.47(18), p.132(59), p.133(60) (61)
Morokawa,Hisashi. p.154(88), p.155(89) (90)
Motohashi, Shigeo. p.92(25)
Numano, Shige. p.33(9), p.45(16), p.139(69)
Pacific Press Service p.137(67), p.160(96) (97) (98), p.161(99)
Scardino, Michael C. p.33(8), p.74(24), p.117(38), p.122(42) (43), p.129(54),
          p.139(68) (70)
Shimauchi, Eisuke. p.127(49) (50), p.129 (51) (53)
Shiotsubo, Mitsuaki. p.90(23), p.141(72), p.142(74), p.143(75) (76) (77) (78)
Soehata, Kaoru. p.135(65)
Sugawara, Kazuhiko. p.78(19), p.88(22), p.94(26), p.141(73)
Takahashi, Fumio p.36(10) (11) (12) (13), p.109 (33)—(36) (37)
Takahashi, Masatomo. p.156(93)
Takamoto, Hiroyuki. p.20(2), p.136 (66)
Takenaka, Fumio. p.151(81), p.152(83)
Wright, Dale R. p.123(46)
Wright, Jody A. p.155(92)
Wuest, Bill p.20(3), p.121(39) (40) (41), p.130(55)
Yajima, Tadashi. p.21(4) (5), p.123(45), p.153(87), p.157(94) (95)
Yoshino, Shin. p.144(79)

Acknowledgements

ABC Leisure Magazine, Inc. p.11
Asahi Sonorama p.166—167
Meredith Corporation p.11
National Geographic Society p.11
Straight Arrow Publishers, Inc. p.11
Board of Education and Governor Livingston Regional High School, Berkeley Heights,
New Jersey p.11
Toshimaen Amusement Park p.43, 75
Yamaha Furniture, Ginza Shop p.30
Ziff-Davis Publishing Company p.11

Credits

p.11:	The cover of Time is reprinted by permission from Time, the weekly news magazine, copyright Time Inc. 1979.
p.11:	© 1979 by The New York Times Company. Reprinted by permission.
p.11:	Issue of Life: Photograph by David Deahl, Life, © 1978, Time Inc.
p.11:	Issue of Newsweek: copyright 1979, by Newsweek Inc. All rights reserved. Reprinted by permission.
p.36:	Kodacolor II, Kodacolor 400, Kodachrome 25, Kodachrome 64, Ektachrome 64, Ektachrome 160, Ektachrome 200, Ektachrome 400 and High Speed Infrared are all registered trademarks of the Eastman Kodak Co.
p.36:	Fujicolor F-II, Fujicolor F-II 400 and Fijichrome 100 are all registered trademarks of the Fuji Film Co.
p.36:	Fotomat and Fotomat 400 are registered trademarks of the Fotomat Co.
p.42:	Unisphere Fountain in Flushing Meadow-Corona Park, City of New York, was designed by the United States Steel Corporation.
p.168(100):	Courtesy of Gernsheim Collection, Humanities Research Center, The University of Texas at Austin.
p.168(101):	Courtesy of Canon Inc.
p.168(102):	Courtesy of the Division of Photographic History, Department of History and Technology, Museum of History and Technology, Smithsonian Institution.
p.168(103):	Courtesy of the Division of Photographic History, Department of History and Technology, Museum of History and Technology, Smithsonian Institution.
p.169(104):	Courtesy of Gernsheim Collection, Humanities Research Center, The University of Texas at Austin.
p.169(105):	Courtesy of Gernsheim Collection, Humanities Research Center, The University of Texas at Austin.
P.169)106):	Courtesy of International Museum of Photography, George Eastman House.
P.169(107):	Courtesy of International Museum of Photography, George Eastman House.